'HATE C RIME AND THE CITY

Paul Iganski

This book is due for return on or before the last date shown below.

This edition published in Great Britain in 2008 by

The Policy Press
University of Bristol
Fourth Floor
Beacon House
Queen's Road
Bristol BS8 1QU
UK

Tel +44 (0)117 331 4054
Fax +44 (0)117 331 4093
e-mail tpp-info@bristol.ac.uk
www.policypress.org.uk

British Library Cataloguing in Publication Data
A catalogue record for this book is available from the British Library.

Library of Congress Cataloging-in-Publication Data
A catalog record for this book has been requested.

ISBN 978 1 86134 939 2 paperback
ISBN 978 1 86134 940 8 hardcover

Cover design by In-Text Design, Bristol.
Cover photo kindly supplied by Jan Dabrowski, www.jdgraphic.com.au
Printed and bound in Great Britain by Henry Ling Ltd, Dorchester.

To Jack Levin, whose inspiration and support
initiated this enterprise

Contents

List of tables and figures

Tables

Figures

Acknowledgements

I wish to thank my former colleagues in the Sociology Department at the University of Essex for covering my duties when I was writing the first draft of this book while on sabbatical leave. I also wish to thank my new colleagues in the Department of Applied Social Science at Lancaster University for the space and encouragement they provided me to complete the final draft of this book. A number of individuals have been particularly helpful. Kevin Armstrong, Jon Garland, Kay Goodall, Jo Goodey, Krista Jansson, Ruth Keen, Vicky Keilinger, Spiridoula Lagou, Gill McIver, Hannah Mason-Bish, Les Moran, Bennett Obong, Susan Paterson, Sue Penna, Barbara Perry, Winston Pickett, Gareth Piggott, Mark Rowland, David Smith, Abe Sweiry, Angela Turton and Alan Weston have either assisted with suggestions and ideas, provided data, or read draft chapters. I also wish to thank the anonymous reviewers who provided helpful comments on earlier drafts of this book. And special thanks go to the Lagou family for the hospitality they provided while the bulk of the draft was being written.

Part of Chapter Two was presented in a paper, 'The banality of antisemitism', to the American Society of Criminology 58th Annual Meeting, Los Angeles, California (2006) and supported by a British Academy Overseas Conference Grant, which the author gratefully acknowledges. Another part of Chapter Two was presented in a lecture 'Hate crime and religious intolerance: lessons from London' at California State University San Bernardino (CSUSB) in May 2007. The author gratefully acknowledges the financial support provided by CSUSB and especially Brian Levin for organising the lecture. Part of Chapter Four was presented in a lecture 'Free to speak, free to hate?' at Old Dominion University (ODU), in November 2006. The author gratefully acknowledges the comments provided by those attending, and especially Victoria Time for organising the lecture, and the financial support provided by ODU.

The data from the British Crime Survey reported in Chapter One and Chapter Four of this book are material from Crown copyright records made available through the Home Office and the UK Data Archive and used by permission of the Controller of Her Majesty's Stationery Office and the Queen's Printer for Scotland. Those who carried out the original analysis and collection of the data bear no responsibility for the further analysis or interpretation provided in this book.

Finally I am very grateful to the staff at The Policy Press, especially Karen Bowler and her predecessor Philip de Bary, and Jo Morton, for their efficiency and support.

ONE

A victim-centred approach to conceptualising 'hate crime'

While it might seem unwise to open a book by picking apart its title, it is a necessary step in unfolding the argument in the following pages. The term 'hate crime' has no legal status in the UK. No law uses the term. Yet the police and other criminal justice agents have enthusiastically embraced it. This has occurred in the decade since the then 'New' Labour government introduced penalty enhancement for racially aggravated offences under section 28 of the 1998 Crime and Disorder Act, the equivalent of the so-called 'hate crime' laws in the US. Such laws provide extra penalties in cases of 'hate crime' compared with similar, but otherwise motivated, crimes (or 'parallel' crimes, as legal scholar Fred Lawrence calls them [1999, p 4]). Even though the term 'hate crime' has caught on in some quarters it is a rather slippery concept. Varying interpretations have been provided in the scholarly and policy literature, but they do have one thing in common: curiously the word 'hate' appears infrequently. Instead, terms such as 'bias', 'prejudice', 'difference' and 'hostility' feature prominently. Furthermore, when the motivating impetus behind so-called 'hate crime' is examined, the emotion of 'hate' often has little to do with the crime in question. In this book the words 'hate crime' are surrounded with single quotation marks to signify that although 'hate' might not often figure in the crimes so-labelled and therefore can be disregarded as an accurate notion of crime, the concept of 'hate crime' is not entirely devoid of utility. Given that this book employs the concept of 'hate crime', this opening chapter explores the conceptual disarray of the notion of 'hate crime' and explains why and how the concept is to be utilised in the book. This chapter makes a case for the victim's experience to be placed at the centre of the conceptualisation of 'hate crime'. A victim–centred approach recognises the salience of the particular harms inflicted by 'hate crimes' compared with parallel crimes, and the chapter introduces evidence of those harms.

Conceptual disarray of the notion of 'hate crime'

'Hate crime' is a misnomer, given the events that the term is used to represent. Over five decades ago Gordon Allport (1954/1979) arguably provided a very clear conceptualisation of 'hate' in his influential book, *The nature of prejudice*, by drawing a distinction between 'hate' and 'anger'. According to Allport, whereas anger 'is a transitory emotional state, aroused by thwarting some ongoing activity', 'hatred [is a] sentiment', not an emotion. It is 'an enduring organization of aggressive impulses toward a person or toward a class of persons. Since it is composed of habitual bitter feeling and accusatory thought, it constitutes a stubborn structure in the mental-emotional life of the individual' (Allport, 1954/1979, p 363). Therefore, in drawing from Allport's conceptualisation, whereas we might think in terms of the 'heat of anger', we might think of 'cold hatred', which is not a transitory mental state, but a resilient inclination of mind. However, if our notion of 'hate crime' is informed solely by Allport's conceptualisation of hatred and its stress on 'aggressive impulses', then 'hate crime' offenders would most likely be confined to the most extreme bigots who either deliberately set out to victimise the targets of their hate or alternatively seize on any opportunity that presents itself to do so. Yet most notably, as Jack Levin and Jack McDevitt demonstrated through their influential typology of 'hate crime' offenders, formulated from their analysis of Boston US police records, extreme hatemongers figure only as a very small minority. Other impulses, such as 'thrill seeking', appeared to Levin and McDevitt more likely to motivate offenders (1993, 1995, 2002).

It is perhaps because of evidence like this that critics such as James B. Jacobs and Kimberly Potter have argued that '"Hate crime" is not really about hate, but about bias or prejudice' (1998, p 11), and 'prejudice', in the view of British scholar Nathan Hall, is an 'entirely different thing' (2005, p 18). This helps us little, however, as 'prejudice', in Jacobs and Potter's view, is a 'complicated, broad and cloudy concept' (1998, p 11). As they point out, most people have some prejudices based either on experience or invention, or from somewhere in between. Some prejudices are favourable in that they are 'for something', some are malign in that they are 'against something', and some are subject to social censure. Some prejudices are also subject to legal censure by so-called 'hate crime' laws when expressed in particular circumstances. What is notable about such laws, however, is that the word 'hate' appears only infrequently. A few examples should help to demonstrate the point.

The US Congress passed the Hate Crime Statistics Act on 23 April 1990 requiring the US Attorney General to collect and annually publish a summary of data on crimes 'that manifest *evidence of prejudice* based on race, religion, sexual orientation, or ethnicity' (emphasis added) (28 USC 534(b)(1)). The list of selected censored prejudices was expanded to include 'disability' by the 1994 Violent Crime Control and Law Enforcement Act. It is notable that, apart from the title of the 1990 Act, the word 'hate' is not used elsewhere in the text of the Act, with 'prejudice' preferred instead.

The 1994 Act added a new twist in highlighting the discriminatory selection of crime victims rather than the animus of the offender, by defining 'hate crime' as 'a crime in which the defendant intentionally selects a victim … *because of* the actual or perceived race, color, religion, national origin, ethnicity, gender, disability, or sexual orientation of any person' (emphasis added) (H.R.3355, Sec 280003). That definition was adopted by the proposed Federal Hate Crime legislation: the 2007 Local Law Enforcement Hate Crimes Prevention Act.

The US Federal Bureau of Investigation, which annually publishes what it calls 'hate crime statistics' as part of its Uniform Crime Reporting (UCR) Program, defines 'hate crime' as 'criminal offenses that are motivated, in whole or in part, by the *offender's bias against* a race, religion, sexual orientation, ethnicity/national origin, or disability and are committed against persons, property or society' (FBI, 2005, p 1; emphasis added). In this case, 'bias' is the preferred term for the motivation associated with the crimes in question. (Lawrence makes the point that: 'I use the term "bias crime" rather than "hate crime" to emphasize that the key factor in a bias crime is not the perpetrator's hatred of the victim per se, but rather his bias or prejudice toward that victim' [1999, p 9].)

If we read the texts of so-called 'hate crime' statutes enacted by many states in the US, we will see similarly that the word 'hate' rarely appears. It is also absent in the 'hate crime' legislation enacted in the UK. (An overview of the legislation is provided in Appendix A of this book.) Following the provisions for racially aggravated offences established by the 1998 Crime and Disorder Act, religiously aggravated offences were created by the 2001 Anti-terrorism, Crime and Security Act. They were a response to the Islamophobic backlash in the UK in the wake of the attacks against the World Trade Center and the Pentagon in the US on 11 September 2001. 'Hate crime' provisions in the UK were extended even further by the 2003 Criminal Justice Act that provides for penalty enhancement in crimes in which the offender demonstrates hostility towards the victim on the basis of sexual orientation or disability. It is notable that in none of these provisions does the word 'hate' appear, and words such as 'prejudice' and 'bias', which are used in the US statutes, are also avoided. Instead, the 1998 Crime and Disorder Act's provisions for 'racially aggravated offences' significantly expanded the lexicon by applying where an offence is motivated to some degree by *hostility* towards members of a racial group, or presumed members of a group, or alternatively where the offender demonstrates hostility based on their victim's membership, or presumed membership, of a racial group, while committing an offence, or immediately before or immediately afterwards. The Home Office (the UK's counterpart to the US Department of Justice) and police forces in the UK have been somewhat less reticent than legislators about using the 'h-word'. For instance, on its website the Home Office states that:

> Hatred is a strong term that goes beyond simply causing offence or hostility. Hate crime is any criminal offence committed against a person or property that is motivated by an *offender's hatred* of someone because of their race, colour, ethnic origin, nationality or national origins; religion; gender, or gender identity; sexual orientation; disability. (www.homeoffice.gov.uk/crime-victims/reducing-crime/hate-crime/, last accessed 3/10/07; emphasis added)

The Association of Chief Police Officers (ACPO) has also not been shy about using the 'h-word'. It defines 'hate crime' as 'Any incident, which constitutes a criminal offence, perceived by the victim or any other person, as being motivated by prejudice or hate' (ACPO, 2005, p 9). ACPO has a similar definition for 'hate incidents' 'which may or may not constitute a criminal offence' (2005, p 9). There has been some equivocation, however, on the part of police forces. For instance, although London's Metropolitan Police Service has what it calls a 'hate crime policy', issued in October 2004, it backtracks on the use of the 'h-word' by very broadly defining a 'hate incident' as an 'incident that is perceived by the victim, or any other person, to be racist, homophobic, transphobic or due to a person's religion, belief, gender identity or disability' (Iganski et al, 2005, p 12).

As can be seen, although it has firmly entered the lexicon of criminal justice, when it comes to the crunch, legislators have shied away from using the 'h-word', relying instead on words such as 'prejudice', 'bias' and 'hostility', which are far less emotive than the word 'hate', but unfortunately only a little less slippery to conceptualise.

'Hate crime' as a scholarly domain

Given the conceptual ambiguities involved, why continue to use the term 'hate crime'? In opening this book it was proposed that the concept of 'hate crime' is not entirely devoid of utility. Chiefly, it has provided an emotive banner under which is now rallied a once disparate field of concerns with oppression and bigotry in various guises. As Jenness and Grattet have argued:

> To those who have promoted and embraced it, the concept
> of hate crime evokes drama, passion, and righteousness, and
> it signifies human tendencies toward tribalism and historic
> challenges to freedom and equality faced by minority
> groups.... A seemingly simple pairing of words – 'hate'
> and 'crime' – creates a signifier that conveys an enormous
> sense of threat and an attendant demand for a response.
> (2001, p 2)

But given the troublesome and ambiguous nexus between 'hate' and 'crime' in the case of so-called 'hate crime', as discussed above, rather than referring to this or that type of crime it is perhaps more pertinent to think of 'hate crime' as a policy domain, an arena in which elements of the political system and criminal justice process have converged and focused on the substantive issue of offences and incidents where some bigotry against the victim plays a part. Jenness and Grattet observed that the foundations of the 'hate crime' policy domain in the US were provided by the activities of the anti-hate crime movement that emerged in the late 1970s, which in turn was built on the strategies of mobilisation of civil rights and victims' rights movements in the 1960s and 1970s. Drawing from the notion of 'hate crime' as a policy domain in which there is a coalition of rights activists, 'hate crime' might also be regarded as a 'scholarly domain' in which there is an analytical coalition between scholars in once disparate fields of study concerned with oppression, discrimination and bigotry in various guises. This is not to propose that previous analyses of racist violence, anti-gay violence and male heterosexual violence against women, for instance, should be re-labelled as 'hate crime' studies. Nor is it to propose that future studies in those fields should be unquestioningly considered as 'hate crime' studies. Instead, conceptualising 'hate crime' as a scholarly domain implies a conversation between scholars rooted in different fields of study and disciplines. This is an analytical conversation distinguished by a focus on the synergies between different forms of oppressive and discriminatory violence, and their intersections where relevant, with respect to the experiences of victims and offenders with a view to informing effective intervention, whether that be the use of the criminal law against, or rehabilitation of, offenders, and support and counselling for victims. It is in the spirit of such an analytical conversation that this book has been written.

The harms of 'hate crime'

In an analysis that subsequently became highly influential for understanding male violence against women, Liz Kelly (1987) proposed over two decades ago that sexual violence could be conceived of as a continuum. Kelly argued that sexual violence is a normal experience for women in that it exists in most women's lives, although the form it takes varies. She also argued that it is a normal part of male heterosexual behaviour. When sexual violence is regarded as a continuum, what distinguishes one form of act from another is not a notion of seriousness in terms of the impact of acts on the women concerned, but rather the relative frequency with which such acts occur. Kelly argued that the reaction of women to sexual violence differs and 'a complex range of factors affect the impact of particular experiences'. Consequently, 'creating a hierarchy of abuse based on seriousness is inappropriate' as 'all forms of sexual violence are serious and have effects: the "more or less" aspect of the continuum refers only to incidence' (Kelly, 1987, p 49).

In the spirit of conceiving of 'hate crime' as a scholarly domain in which there is an analytical conversation between once disparate fields of study, Kelly's way of thinking about acts of violence against women can be utilised for the conceptualisation 'hate crime' more broadly. What distinguishes one form of act from another is not any notion of relative seriousness about acts in terms of the impact on victims because, as Kelly observed, a complex range of factors impact on the particular experiences of victims. However, what distinguishes 'hate crime' from other types of crime is that all 'hate crimes' generally hurt more than parallel crimes. The notion that 'hate crimes' inflict greater harms on their victims is therefore the fundamental dimension in its conceptualisation. The evidence behind this assertion will be explored in depth in Chapter Four of this book. Here, a snapshot is presented in the case of racist incidents, by using evidence from the British Crime Survey (BCS) to make the point about greater harm being key to the conceptualisation of 'hate crime'. Even though it is a 'snapshot', the evidence goes beyond much that can be found to date in the literature on racist violence in the UK.

The BCS samples the experiences of adults aged 16 and over in households living in private residential accommodation in England and Wales. The survey includes a 'non-White' boost sample as the number of respondents from Black and Asian minority ethnic communities would otherwise be insufficient, given their small representation in the population of England and Wales, to enable a robust analysis of their specific experiences. (Even the boost sample in any one-year's sweep of the survey provides insufficient numbers of minority ethnic respondents for a rigorous analysis. Consequently, the data used in the discussion that follows combine three annual sweeps of the BCS for 2002/03, 2003/04 and 2004/05.) Respondents were asked screening questions early on in the survey interview about whether they themselves, or a member of their current household, had been a victim of a 'crime or offence' within the 12 months before the date of the interview, and if they had, on how many occasions. To prompt their memory they were asked about a range of offences in turn, from theft and damage to a motor vehicle, bicycle theft, burglary, theft from a person, threats and violence. In the case of threats, for instance, respondents were asked, 'Has anyone threatened to damage things of yours or threatened to use force or violence in any way that actually frightened you?'. In the case of assault the respondent was asked, 'Has anyone, including people you know well, deliberately hit you with their fists or a weapon of any sort or kicked you or used force or violence in any way?'.

More detailed questions were asked about all of the incidents reported in response to the screening questions, including whether they believed that the reported incidents were 'racially motivated'. Unfortunately, respondents were not asked if they thought incidents occurred because of the victim's sexual orientation, their religion, or because of a disability that they might have. Therefore the analysis here is necessarily confined to incidents that were perceived to be racially motivated. (The BCS has included a question since 2005/06 on whether victims of crime thought the incident was religiously motivated. A question was also introduced on an experimental basis in the 2007/08 BCS to ask whether crimes were perceived to be motivated on account of the victim's sexual orintation, disability or age. To date, however, there are insufficient sweeps of the BCS with these questions included to enable a robust analysis.)

The majority of incidents reported in the survey were 'one-off' events. However, in a substantial minority of cases, respondents reported being victimised more than once. If a respondent reported more than six incidents in the 12 months prior to the interview, and they were different types of incidents, the incidents were prioritised in order and only the first six in the order of priority were followed up with detailed questions. If a person experienced the same type of incident more than once the incidents were classified as a 'series': defined as 'the same thing, done under the same circumstances and probably by the same people' (Grant et al, 2006, p 19). In such cases, detailed questions were asked only about the most recent incident in the series.

It is instructive to briefly note first some descriptive observations about the reported racially motivated incidents to set the context for the data on the harms of such incidents that follow. Incidents were reported by respondents from each of the minority ethnic groups and the White groups. However, the proportions reported by respondents from the Black and Asian minority ethnic groups greatly exceed the White groups (see Table 1.1).

Table 1.1: Percentage of incidents believed to be racially motivated, by ethnic group (Row %)

	% of all incidents believed to be racially motivated	All incidents reported (n)
Mixed–White and Black Caribbean	12.2	378
Mixed–White and Black African	24.8	141
Mixed–White and Asian	11.1	207
Mixed–Any Other Mixed Background	7.9	290
Asian or Asian British–Indian	13.9	1,899
Asian or Asian British–Pakistani	16.7	1,380
Asian or Asian British–Bangladeshi	19.4	360
Asian or Asian British–Other Asian Background	16.4	567
Black or Black British–Caribbean	7.6	1,215
Black or Black British–African	13.7	1,056
Black or Black British–Other Black Background	12.0	108
Chinese	12.1	257
Other Ethnic Group	10.2	787
White British	0.8	52,557
White Irish	1.5	600
Other White Background	3.5	2,161

Notes: The table uses data from variables Ethnic, RaceMot and NumInc. Numbers of incidents include all 'one-off' incidents and up to the first five where there are a series of incidents. The data exclude incidents where respondents answered 'Other', 'Don't know' or declined to answer.
Source: BCS 2002/03, 2003/04 and 2004/05

Most starkly, almost one in five crime incidents reported by 'Asian or Asian British–Bangladeshi' respondents, for instance, were believed to be racially motivated compared with less than one in a hundred incidents reported by 'White British' respondents.

The idea that people from the White community could be victims of racist violence has been strongly contested and it would be no exaggeration to suggest that the scholarly literature and research on racist violence in the UK has almost entirely conceptualised the problem in terms of White offenders and Black and minority ethnic victims. In the very few instances in the literature where incidents against the White group are considered, the 'race-hate' context of incidents is downplayed. For instance, Eugene McLaughlin has argued that:

> In the UK, in the aftermath of the publication of the Macpherson report, police officers now accept that 'a racist incident is any incident which is perceived to be racist by the victim or any other person'. There is evidence that police officers and white residents in certain neighbourhoods, as part of a backlash, are interpreting virtually any conflictual encounter with non-whites as a 'race-hate' act and thereby reporting it as such. Hence, we are witnessing, through the mobilization of white resentments, a determined effort to subvert the meaning and purpose of the new policy on racial incidents. (McLaughlin, 2002, p 495)

Even though McLaughlin does not cite any of the 'evidence' to which he refers, Hall subsequently echoes the assertion (Hall, 2005, p 200). However, the report of the Inquiry into the murder of Stephen Lawrence acknowledged, in a passage that has been little cited in the volumes of commentary on the Inquiry, that 'Racist prejudice and stereotyping can work and be evident both ways. In the search for justice, and in the quest for better relationship between the Police Services and minority ethnic communities this must be firmly borne in mind. Racism either way must be treated with zero tolerance' (Macpherson, 1999, para 45.25). Yet the problem of whether White people can be victims of 'race-hate' crime has been dogged by controversy in the UK ever since the 1981 Home Office report *Racial attacks*, hailed as putting 'racial attacks on the political agenda for the first time' (Home Office, 1989, p 1), used a working definition of a 'racial incident' as an 'inter-racial incident', defined as: 'An incident, or alleged offence by a person or persons of one racial group against a person or persons or property of another racial group, where there are indications of a racial motive' (Home Office, 1981, p 7, para 20). This definition clearly allows for people from the White group to be victims of racial incidents as evidenced by the data presented on such incidents in the Home Office report. Critics of the report, such as Paul Gordon, argued that 'to claim, in the absence of any evidence, that attacks by black people on white people are "racial", is to render the concept of racism quite meaningless' (Gordon, 1986, p 5). Gordon argued that from the working definition of racial incidents used by the Home Office, 'It is difficult to read this as meaning anything other than that the government was not prepared to recognize the phenomenon of racism which underlies such attacks, or the context of such attacks where the racist attack acts both as a reflection and a reinforcer of the racism institutionalized in society' (Gordon, 1986, p 2). If interpretations of racial attacks are solely contextualised with respect to prevailing structures of dominance at the societal level, then attacks against the White group do indeed present a conundrum. This will be returned to in Chapter Three, and in the analysis that follows the experiences of White victims as reported in the BCS will be placed alongside the experiences of minority ethnic victims as the data informs the discussion in question in that chapter.

To turn from one contentious matter to another, a prominent criticism of crime victimisation surveys is that they provide a static and 'decontextualised' picture of crime that conceals the processes behind incidents (cf Bowling, 1993). The BCS provides just a small insight into the processual dynamics of many racially motivated incidents as the data show that such incidents were more likely, for the minority ethnic and White groups alike, to be part of a series of incidents compared with those incidents that were not believed to be racially motivated (see Table 1.2). The extent of repeat victimisation was slightly greater for the minority ethnic groups combined compared with the White group for the racially motivated incidents.

Some victims based their judgement about racial motivation on the appearance of the offender (their 'race/country of origin') and the proportion of White victims making their judgement in this way was twice as high as the proportion of minority ethnic victims (see Table 1.3). Another of the prime indicators of racial motivation was racist language used by the offender. Such language was reported by a higher proportion of minority ethnic victims than people from the White group.

A dominant argument in support of so-called 'hate crime' laws in the US is the assertion that they hurt more than similar but otherwise motivated crimes. However, as will be discussed in Chapter Four, much of the evidence to date behind this assertion has been somewhat

Table 1.2: Percentage of reported incidents that were the most recent in a series of incidents: racially motivated compared with non-racially motivated (Row %)

	Racially motivated		Non-racially motivated	
	Series (%)	All incidents (n)	Series (%)	All incidents (n)
Mixed–White and Black Caribbean	45.5*	22	20.2	247
Mixed–White and Black African	53.3**	15	16.9	83
Mixed–White and Asian	41.7*	12	13.4	149
Mixed–Any Other Mixed Background	30.8	13	23.5	179
Asian or Asian British–Indian	31.9***	160	15.5	1,298
Asian or Asian British–Pakistani	35.6***	132	17.5	868
Asian or Asian British–Bangladeshi	28.9	45	17.1	222
Asian or Asian British–Other Asian Background	30.9**	55	13.5	392
Black or Black British–Caribbean	27.6*	58	16.4	884
Black or Black British–African	28.9***	97	13.3	753
Black or Black British–Other Black Background	0.0	13	13.3***	75
Chinese	31.3	16	12.4	185
Other Ethnic Group	21.4	56	12.7	575
White British/Irish/Other White Background	28.8***	302	17.5	41,320

Notes: The table uses data from variables Ethnic, RaceMot and Pincid. The data exclude incidents where respondents answered 'Other', 'Don't know' or declined to answer.
*$p<0.05$, **$p<0.01$, ***$p<0.001$
Source: BCS 2002/03, 2003/04 and 2004/05

equivocal. Evidence from the BCS, in the case of racially motivated incidents, appears to show that 'hate crimes' do indeed hurt more (Iganski, 2001), and consequently the greater harm involved provides the common denominator for the conceptualisation of 'hate crime'. It was noted above that in the case of sexual violence Kelly (1987) proposed that what distinguishes one form of act from another is not a notion of seriousness in terms of the impact of the acts on the women concerned, but rather the relative frequency with which such acts occur. This proposition can be applied to thinking about the racially motivated incidents reported by the BCS. To take one indicator of

Table 1.3: Reasons given by victims for believing incidents to be racially motivated (%)[a]

	Minority ethnic groups	White groups
Racist language	48.4	36.6
Victim's race/country of origin	50.9	36.3
Offender's race/country of origin	14.4	29.5
Offence only committed against minorities	11.0	2.8
Some people pick on minorities	17.1	7.1
Has happened before	20.6	18.0
Other	9.5	15.8
Total number of racially motivated incidents	703	322

Notes: [a] Cumulative percentages are greater than 100% as respondents could select all responses that applied. The data in this table, and those that follow in this chapter, include incidents that occurred outside England and Wales.
The table uses data from variables Ethnic, RaceMot and YRaceMoA – YRaceMol. The data exclude incidents where respondents answered 'Don't know' or declined to answer.

Source: BCS 2002/03, 2003/04 and 2004/05

potential harm – the emotional impact of crime – respondents were asked whether they had an 'emotional reaction' following an incident. For each of the major types of crime reported it is notable that higher proportions of victims who believed that incidents were racially motivated reported an emotional reaction compared with victims of incidents that were not believed to be racially motivated (see Table 1.4).

Table 1.4: Percentage of respondents reporting emotional reactions after incidents by offence type: racially motivated compared with non-racially motivated incidents, minority ethnic and White groups combined (Row %)

Type of crime (Home Office code)	Racially motivated incidents		Non-racially motivated incidents	
	%	n	%	n
Assault and attempted assault	92.4*	262	86.8	3717
Robbery and theft from person	91.8	49	88.7	2,264
Burglary and attempted burglary	97.3***	37	84.3	6,267
Theft and attempted theft	91.9***	74	82.8	17,892
Criminal damage	93.9***	228	86.6	11,481
Threats	91.2*	294	88.0	3,343

Notes: The table uses data from variables Ethnic, RaceMot, EmotReac and Offence (recoded). The data exclude incidents where respondents answered 'Other', 'Don't know' or declined to answer.
$*p<0.05$, $**p<0.01$, $***p<0.001$
Source: BCS 2002/03, 2003/04 and 2004/05

Table 1.5: Respondents reporting being affected 'very much': racially motivated compared with non-racially motivated incidents (Row %)

| | Minority ethnic groups | | | | Whites | | | |
| | Racially motivated | | Non-racially motivated | | Racially motivated | | Non-racially motivated | |
	%	n	%	n	%	n	%	n
Assault/ attempted assault	51.8	164	44.8	328	41.0*	78	29.4	2,896
Robbery/snatch theft/theft from person	59.3**	27	36	456	38.9	18	23.2	1,551
Burglary/ attempted burglary/theft in dwelling	88.5***	26	37.4	685	90.0***	10	27.3	4,595
Theft/attempted theft	50.9***	53	24.2	2,090	53.3**	15	17.5	12,711
Criminal damage	56.2***	169	22.8	1,004	34.1*	44	17.9	8,939
Threats	40.1	172	35.9	262	29.2	96	23.7	2,674

Notes: The table uses data from variables Ethnic, RaceMot, HowAff1 and Offence (recoded). The data exclude incidents where respondents answered 'Other', 'Don't know' or declined to answer.
*p<0.05, **p<0.01, ***p<0.001
Source: BCS 2002/03, 2003/04 and 2004/05

The pattern of greater harm holds for the Black and Asian minority ethnic groups combined and the White groups combined, with stronger emotional reactions consistently reported for racially motivated incidents (see Table 1.5).

From extreme to everyday 'hate crime'

If our knowledge about 'hate crime' was confined to what we read in the national newspapers or what we saw on the television news then the impression that we would be most likely left with is that victims are usually targeted in premeditated violent attacks by offenders who are out-and-out bigots, hate-fuelled individuals, who subscribe to racist, antisemitic, homophobic and other bigoted views, and exercise their extreme hatred against their victims. The drama of extreme 'hate' is news, and news reporting generally spotlights the most violent incidents. Tragically, there has been no shortage of such newsworthy incidents. Paul Gordon, in his 1986 Runnymede Research Report, *Racial violence and harassment*, lists 62 murders in Britain between 1970 and 1985 that were either known, or, as Gordon pointed out, were 'widely believed within the black community', to be motivated by 'race hate' (Gordon, 1986, p 8). The murders continued into the 1990s, and the most widely publicised killings included the stabbing to death of 15-year-old Rolan Adams by a gang of youths calling themselves the 'Nazi Turn Outs' in Thamesmead, South London in 1991. In 1992, 16-year-old Rohit Duggal was stabbed to death by a White youth in Eltham, South London, in what is widely believed to be a racist attack. In the same area, the following year Stephen Lawrence was stabbed to death in the street. Covert filming of suspects revealed their extreme racist views and their inclination towards violence. In 1994, 17-year-old Shah Alam was attacked by a group of White youths in Poplar, in the London Borough of Tower Hamlets. He was hit with a hammer, punched, kicked and stabbed, and left for dead on the ground. He was fortunate to survive, following emergency surgery. One of his attackers was heard to shout: "Paki", "Kill him", "Get out of the country". In 1997, 20-year-old Brunel University student Ricky Reel was found dead in the River Thames after disappearing following an incident in which he was racially abused on the street during a night out with friends in Kingston upon Thames, south-west London. The coroner's inquest recorded an open verdict on his death. In another extreme incident in London in 1999, the Admiral Duncan, a 'gay pub' in Soho, was bombed by David Copeland, a young man with a history of involvement with racist groups. Three died, and many more were injured. Copeland, who hoped to spark a 'race war' (cf McLagan and Lowles, 2000), was also responsible for nail bombings in Brixton and Whitechapel in London that did not result in fatalities, but left many injured. In another case in London that made the national news because of the brutality involved, 24-year-old Jody Dobrowski was beaten to death on Clapham Common in South London in October 2005, in what prosecutors alleged was a 'premeditated plan to attack a gay man'. According to a report in *The Times*, 'the killers could be heard by witnesses screaming anti-gay insults as they beat the barman to death' (see 'Two face 30 years in jail for homophobic murder', *The Times*, 13 May 2006: www.timesonline.co.uk/article/0,,29389-2177999,00.html). The two men who were convicted for the crime and who – according to the police officers who first arrived at the crime scene – had beaten their victim to a 'bloody swollen pulp', were each sentenced to a minimum of 28 years in prison (see 'Men jailed for gay barman murder', *BBC News*, 16 June 2006: http://news.bbc.co.uk/1/hi/england/london/5087286.stm). That same year, 18-year-old Black student, Anthony Walker, was murdered with an ice axe in a racially motivated attack in Huyton, Merseyside. His attackers, two cousins, were sentenced to serve a minimum of 23 and 17 years respectively for his murder (see www.liverpoolecho.co.uk/liverpool-news/liverpool-campaigns/anthony-walker/p6/). In June 2006 50-year-old Rikki Judkins, who had learning difficulties, was killed in an attack in Lancaster city centre which culminated with a rock being dropped on his head. Disability rights campaigners believe that he was targeted because of his learning difficulties. A 20-year-old man and a 16-year-old teenager were sentenced to 'life' for the murder (http://news.bbc.co.uk/1/hi/england/lancashire/6369319.stm). In August 2007, 23-year-old disabled man Brent Martin was beaten to death 'for fun' in Sunderland. Although his killers received 'life' sentences (Burton, 2008), disability rights campaigners were disappointed that the judge did not point out that the murder was aggravated on account of Brent Martin's disability.

But news media reporting of incidents of extreme violence, such as those just catalogued, paints an inaccurate picture of the prevailing state of 'hate crime', as the media does with crime in general: the 'dramatic fallacy', in the words of Marcus Felson (2002, p 1). Behind the reported incidents of extreme violence are literally thousands upon thousands of incidents of 'hate crime' that occur each year that do not make the news, ranging from assaults, to criminal damage, to verbal abuse and harassment. Arguably, the scholarly and policy literature has been more preoccupied with the dramatic than everyday incidents, and in the mainland European academic literature on racist attacks against immigrants, refugees and asylum seekers there is something of a tradition in framing analysis of the problem in terms of organised violence from the extreme right and by neo-Nazi skinheads (cf Björgo and Witte, 1993; Björgo, 1995; van Donselar and Wagenaar, 2007) even though it has been shown that they account for only a minority of incidents. Texts produced by US scholars also generally contain the seemingly obligatory chapter on far right perpetrators of 'hate crime' (cf Perry, 2001; Levin and McDevitt, 2002; Gerstenfeld and Grant, 2004).

There is a paucity of official data on the types of 'hate crime' committed in the UK and it is instructive therefore to again examine a snapshot of data from the BCS. The data are revealing, because, as Table 1.6 shows, according to the victims' accounts, offenders used force or physical violence in only a minority of incidents.

Table 1.6: Percentage of reported racially motivated incidents in which the offender used force or violence (Row %)

	Incidents involving force or violence (%)	All racially motivated incidents (n)
Against minority ethnic groups	33.1	703[a]
Against Whites	42.2	322[a]

Notes: [a] Excludes the small number of respondents who answered 'Don't know'.
The table uses data from variables Ethnic, RaceMot, V710 and UseForce.

Source: BCS 2002/03, 2003/04 and 2004/05

This is not to minimise in any way the experiences of victims – in one third of incidents in which force or violence was used, victims were punched or slapped, and in a third of violent incidents the victims were grabbed or pushed. These are all highly distressing and threatening experiences (see Table 1.7).

Overall, however, the physical harms inflicted were relatively few in relation to the total number of incidents. For those incidents in which force or violence was used, the most commonly reported injury was 'minor bruising or black eye' (see Table 1.8).

Table 1.7: Types of force or violence used in racially motivated incidents (Column %)[a]

	Minority ethnic victims (%)	White victims (%)
Grabbed or pulled my bag	5.9	5.5
Grabbed or pushed me	35.0	31.5
Punched or slapped me	35.0	42.5
Kicked me	16.8	26.0
Hit me with a weapon	10.9	20.5
Sexually assaulted me	0.9	3.1
Verbal abuse	44.1	33.9
Other	15.0	8.7
Total number of incidents in which force or violence was used	220	127

Notes: [a] Cumulative percentages are greater than 100% as respondents could select as many responses as applied.
The table uses data from variables Ethnic, RaceMot and WhatForA-WhatForL.

Source: BCS 2002/03, 2003/04 and 2004/05

Table 1.8: Injuries reported by victims of racially motivated incidents (Column %)

	Ethnic minorities (%)	Whites (%)
Minor bruising or black eye	6.7	9.0
Severe bruising	4.0	8.1
Scratches	2.4	3.7
Cuts	4.6	4.7
Broken bones	0.6	0.6
Broken nose	0.4	–
Broken/lost teeth	0.3	0.3
Chipped teeth	0.1	0.9
Concussion or loss of consciousness	1.0	0.6
Other	0.9	1.2
All reported racially motivated incidents (n)	703	322

Note: The table uses data from variables Ethnic, RaceMot and WhInjuA-WhInjuL
Source: BCS 2002/03, 2003/04 and 2004/05

From the background to the foreground of 'hate crime'

The UK's adaptation of 'hate crime' laws, first initiated by the provisions for racially aggravated offences under the 1998 Crime and Disorder Act, brings the potential for more comprehensively understanding the dynamics of 'hate crime'. It is that potential that this book tries to seize. The well-chosen word 'hostility', which needs to be manifest by offenders on account of their victims' 'race', ethnicity, religion, sexual orientation or disability, for them to fall foul of the law in the UK, encompasses a far greater range of sentiments and behaviour than conveyed by the highly emotive and charged word 'hate'. As Horvath and Kelly (2007) have recently argued, hate 'violence does not occur because those committing the violence "hate" the victim but because they belong, or are thought to belong, to a specified social group' (2007, p 5). Yet there are reasons why the violence occurs on account of the victim's group identity, or putative group identity. The offender is arguably acting out and conveying deleterious notions of difference about the 'Other', of which their victim is the embodiment, in situations where the offender exercises, or tries to exercise, power over their victim. Barbara Perry (2001) has very aptly conceptualised this process as 'doing difference'. It is arguably this process that the word 'hostility' in the UK 'hate crime' laws signifies, a process not conveyed by the neutral words 'bias' and 'prejudice' that have been favoured by legislators and scholars in the US. While the term 'hate crime', it has been argued, pathologises acts of violence as the product of 'individual psychology' (cf Horvath and Kelly, 2007, p 4), the notion of 'doing difference' grounds the acts in question in societal conceptions of the 'Other'. From this perspective, acts of 'hate crime' are rooted in ideological structures of societal oppression that are marked by 'deeply embedded notions of difference' (Perry, 2001, p 46), concerning 'race', ethnicity, gender, sexuality, disability and class. These notions of difference are characterised by negative, deviant, inferior evaluations of the 'Other' relative to the dominant norm, and they serve to legitimise acts of violence against the 'Other'. According to Perry, 'Members of subordinate groups are potential victims *because of* their subordinate status. They already are deemed inferior, deviant, and therefore deserving of whatever hostility and persecution comes their way' (Perry, 2001, p 56). By their actions 'hate crime' offenders are not only acting out these notions of difference: they are also at the same time reconstructing the prevailing structures of oppression and reinforcing the boundaries of difference. As Perry argues, through the gaze of key perspectives central to 'structured action theory', the 'distinction between structure and action is a false one'. Consequently, again in Perry's words, 'human action and interaction within these structural contexts are not merely determined; they are also determinant. Structures of domination are both context and outcome, constitutive of and by human behaviour and interaction' (Perry, 2001, p 53).

Perry argues that 'hate crime' is an 'apolitical' term that fails to convey the structural, cultural and ideological underpinnings of the actions to which the label refers. It neutralises appreciation of the power relations behind those actions. By casting racist, homophobic, gendered and other acts of violence and crime in terms of the sentiment of 'hate', the label 'hate crime' also individualises the problem as the abnormal and pathological behaviour of severely bigoted individuals. As Perry argues: 'To pathologize hate is to present it as irrational, as the product of a sick mind' (Perry, 2005, p 125). Given the structural underpinnings of 'hate crime', however, it can be seen as entirely normal behaviour. From the way that offenders see their world, it is 'rational': it is about the assertion of the offender's 'own identity and belongingness over and above others – in short, about power' (Perry, 2005, p 125). From this perspective, Perry argues that:

There is nothing irrational or pathological about engaging
in racist violence, for example, in a decidedly racist culture. It
is, rather, wholly rational given the array of institutionalized
practices and discourses that lend permission to minimize or
victimize the Others in our midst. Hate crime is nested in a
web of everyday practices that are used to marginalize and
disempower targeted communities. (Perry, 2005, p 126)

Barbara Perry's theoretical perspectives raise a fundamental question
about whether 'hate crime' offenders are consciously and instrumentally
'doing difference'. Although she does not seem explicitly to state
it often, her analysis does make clear that 'hate crime' is *'intended to
marginalize'* (Perry, 2001, p 214; emphasis added), and *'intended* to sustain
somewhat precarious hierarchies, through violence and threats of
violence (verbal or physical)' (Perry, 2001, p 3; emphasis added). It is
clear from her writings that Perry characterises 'hate crime' as purposive,
intentional behaviour on the part of offenders: '[I]t is a mechanism of
power and oppression, intended to reaffirm the precarious hierarchies
that characterize a given social order. It is intended to simultaneously
recreate the threatened (real or imagined) hegemony of the perpetrator's
group, and the "appropriate" subordinate identity of the victim's group'
(Perry, 2005, p 128).

However, it would be fair to observe that empirical evidence to
support the claim of purposive instrumentalism behind the actions
of 'hate crime' offenders is not offered by Perry in her analysis, and
this point is critical to the analysis offered in Chapter Two of this
book. While she argues that, because of the symbiotic relationship
involved, the 'structure–action' distinction is false, Perry does not go
on to illuminate the chain of connection between structural context
and the actions of 'hate crime' offenders.

Appreciation of the structural context behind acts of 'hate crime'
alone does not adequately provide an understanding of the lived reality
of 'hate crime' as experienced by victims and offenders. If, as Jacobs
and Potter contend (1998, p 11), everybody harbours some prejudice
of some kind, the pressing question for understanding 'hate crime' is
what brings some people in particular circumstances to express their
prejudices against others in criminal acts. To answer this question, and
to better understand the nexus between background structure and
the foreground of 'hate crime', we arguably need to begin with the
social situational circumstances of offending. Such a focus provides the
primary concern of Chapter Two, and the dominant theme pursued
across the chapter is that 'hate crime' often occurs in the context of

the unfolding of the everyday and ordinary lives of the offenders, and it often occurs when a particular situation provides the opportunity for, or impels, the expression of their bigotry. The 1998 Crime and Disorder Act's provision that hostility can be an aggravating element, accompanying, but not necessarily driving, offences, reflects more inclusively the day-to-day reality of how bigotry is manifest in the lives of offenders and their victims. 'Hate' clearly fuels the actions of the extreme bigot on occasion, but again, arguably, far more numerous are the occasions where bigotry surfaces not by design, but when an opportunity or a provocation occurs, as Chapter Two demonstrates. Given these perspectives, those analyses that focus on the background structural, cultural and political underpinnings of 'hate crime' are literally looking at the problem from back to front. Examining events the other way round, by starting with the lived experience of 'hate crime', paradoxically sheds light on the background factors, and importantly it also begins to illuminate the inside of the 'black box' (Katz, 1988, p 5) between context and action, whereas a sole concern with the background cannot begin to lift the lid off that box.

Conclusion: situating the victim at the centre of 'hate crime'

This chapter has argued for the victim to be placed at the centre of the conceptualisation of 'hate crime'. Given the ambiguous and often uncertain nexus between 'hate' and crime in cases of so-called 'hate crime', the one common characteristic that we can be sure about is that 'hate crimes' hurt more than parallel crimes: this is borne out by the experiences of victims. What those experiences also show is that, contrary to media depictions of the problem, many incidents of 'hate crime' are not committed by extremist bigots, do not involve premeditated attacks by thugs who are predisposed to violence, often do not involve physical violence at all, and in many instances do not involve 'hate'. Instead, many incidents are committed by 'ordinary' people in the context of their 'everyday' lives. Chapter Two demonstrates this through a victim-centred approach by unravelling the situational dynamics of incidents as reported by victims. As well as providing an understanding of the foreground of incidents, unravelling the situational dynamics of incidents, as will be argued in the chapter, illuminates the background structural contexts in which 'hate crimes' occur and helps understanding of the relationship between background structure and offender action.

In Chapter Three it is noted that the few studies that have focused on the spatial aspects of 'racist attacks' show that the geography of space and place clearly matters in terms of mediating between the background structural contexts of incidents and the foreground experience of offending and victimisation. Consequently, the chapter explores the spatial dynamics of victims' experiences of 'hate crime' using previously unpublished statistical data on incidents provided by London's Metropolitan Police Service.

Chapter Four examines in depth the harms of 'hate crime' as experienced by victims by using data from the BCS. The chapter draws on the data to offer new perspectives on the longstanding debate about the desirability of 'hate crime' laws. As will be discussed in the chapter, the punitive sanctions introduced by such laws might be viewed in some quarters as being an unwelcome case of the decline of 'penal welfarism' and correctionalism and the rise of punitive and expressive justice (Garland, 2001). However, the provision of equal concern and respect for all people, and respect for difference – principles that provide the motivating impetus for advocates of 'hate crime' laws – constitute a central plank of political liberalism. And against those who have argued that 'hate crime' laws use illiberal means to achieve liberal ends, it is argued in the chapter that the harsher punishment of 'hate crime' offenders compared with offenders in parallel crimes seems to be justified by the liberal principle of proportionate sentencing and provides offenders with their just deserts, given the strength of the evidence that 'hate crimes' inflict greater harms than parallel crimes.

Given the centrality of the victim to the conceptualisation of 'hate crime', Chapter Five focuses on the significance of including the victim in the 'hate crime' policy process. The chapter elaborates findings from research carried out by the author on the London-wide Race Hate Crime Forum in 2006 and 2007 (Iganski, 2007) to illuminate and evaluate efforts to include victims of racist crime in multi-agency working at the London-wide level. The chapter draws out the tensions involved in confronting criminal justice agents with the experiences of victims and also the problem of competing claims by different groups of victims for inclusion in the policy process.

The concluding chapter, Chapter Six, draws out the synergies, but also the divergences, between some key themes in the analysis presented in the book and elements of the 'criminologies of everyday life' (Garland, 2002). One key point of departure involves the argument in the book for the critical role of the state in intervening against potential 'hate crime' offenders. It is argued that the persistence and the ubiquity of the value systems that underpin acts of 'hate crime' provide the need for the law to serve as a cue against potential transgression. 'Hate crime' laws are consequently an explicit attack on the background structure that provides the context for the motivating impulses in acts of 'hate crime'. Such laws are intended ultimately to reweave the structural fabric by legislating morality. However, given that the problem of 'hate crime' has been framed as a human rights problem, state intervention, when it legislates against 'hate', involves the state either as the guarantor or alternatively the violater of the human rights of its citizens, depending upon which perspective is taken. In this vein, the chapter concludes by exploring the clash of rights involved in the troubling nexus between 'hate crime' and 'hate speech'.

TWO

The normality of everyday 'hate crime'

A recent report for the US-based international human rights organisation, Human Rights First, argued that the most pervasive and most threatening form of racist violence in Europe and North America 'is also perhaps the most banal and unorganized: the low-level violence of the broken window, the excrement through the letter box, late night banging on doors, and the pushes, kicks and blows delivered to the passerby on the sidewalk' (McClintock, 2005, p 5). While issue might be taken with the notion that any such incidents can be 'low level' (on this matter see also Chahal and Julienne, 1999, p 8), given the evidence of the emotional impacts of 'hate crime' discussed in Chapter One (and to be dealt with further in Chapter Four), victims' experiences do show that such incidents are indeed pervasive and ordinary, and not unusual. By the same token, the experiences of victims also show us that in general 'hate crime' offenders are not an aberration, or politically motivated extremists confined to the margins of society. Instead, many are 'ordinary' people who offend in the unfolding contexts of their everyday lives. The ordinariness of offenders and offending is arguably a further key dimension in the conceptualisation of 'hate crime' (in addition to the dimension of harm as proposed in Chapter One), when victims' experiences are placed at the centre of understanding about 'hate crime'. This line of argument is pursued in this chapter in the spirit of conceptualising 'hate crime' as a scholarly domain characterised by an analysis of the commonalities and differences between various forms of oppressive violence. In that spirit it unravels the situational dynamics of anti-Jewish, anti-Muslim and other racist incidents, incidents against people with a disability and homophobic incidents. It will be argued that understanding the situational foreground of incidents is not only important in its own right for understanding how and why incidents occur, but it also sheds light on the background structural contexts that inform the actions of offenders. And, most significantly, it illuminates the connections between background structure and the foreground of offender action in cases of 'hate crime', providing the missing link between the macro-societal ideological edifice and the micro-level actions of offenders.

The commonalities of everyday 'hate crime'

To begin to unfold the reasoning presented in this chapter it is very instructive to take anti-Jewish incidents first, even though they are relatively few in number compared with the overall incidence of racist crime. This is because for a while it was recently accepted wisdom in policy circles and among some commentators that the majority of anti-Jewish incidents were being perpetrated by extremists and were a manifestation of political violence against Jewish people, not by ordinary people in the context of their everyday lives. There is a good prima facie case for such a view as upsurges in incidents against Jewish people commonly correspond with media reporting of upsurges in the Israel–Palestine conflict, and other conflicts in the Middle East more widely.

According to the 'extremism thesis', in addition to the longstanding involvement of far right extremists in incidents, and the more recent involvement of radical Islamists, attacks against Jews have reputedly *in the main* been perpetrated by 'Arab' or 'Muslim' youths, venting their hatred against Israel and against Jewish people in general. A sharp rise in incidents against Jews that occurred in some European countries in April 2002, corresponding with the Israel Defence Force actions in Jenin on the West Bank, prompted the European Union Monitoring Centre (EUMC) (now named the European Agency for Fundamental Rights [FRA]) to investigate the phenomenon – the first time that it had specifically focused on anti-Jewish incidents since it was established in 1997. However, in the report published it concluded that 'the majority' of attacks 'were carried out by far right extremists whose political agenda is the intimidation of ethnic minorities, not the criticism of Israel's perceived human rights abuses. Nevertheless, the climate of hostility towards Israel provides such groups with a convenient cover' (EUMC, 2004, p 208). Almost a year later, the US Department of State's *Report on global anti-Semitism* added 'Muslim youths' into the cocktail of offenders, by arguing that:

> In Western Europe, traditional far-right groups still account for a significant proportion of the attacks against Jews and Jewish properties; disadvantaged and disaffected Muslim youths increasingly were responsible for most of the other incidents. This trend appears likely to persist as the number of Muslims in Europe continues to grow while their level of education and economic prospects remain limited. (US Department of State, 2005)

At present, police forces in few European countries routinely collect, analyse and publish data on anti-Jewish incidents. Consequently the claims just discussed about the perpetrators of incidents have rested on arguably tenuous data. The first published police data on anti-Jewish incidents in the UK presented an analysis of Metropolitan Police Service data for 2001–04, reported in *Hate crimes against London's Jews* (Iganski et al, 2005), and they paint a different picture than that painted by the 'extremism thesis'. The reported quantitative data on incidents are limited but illuminating nevertheless, in terms of providing an insight into offenders: the majority of recorded suspects (83.4%) were male; the age range of suspects is skewed towards the lower age ranges – as is the case for crime suspects in general – with the largest proportion of suspects aged 16–20; and where information was available about the ethnic appearance of suspects, based on the victim's perception and information from witnesses, just over half (56.9%) of suspects were classified as 'White European'.

The profile of suspected perpetrators of anti-Jewish incidents in London is similar to Manchester in north-west England, where Britain's second largest Jewish community is located. According to data from the Greater Manchester Police provided in a submission made to the All-Party Parliamentary Inquiry into Antisemitism in 2006 (All-Party Parliamentary Group Against Antisemitism, 2006a), the majority of suspected offenders in incidents recorded over a two-year period from December 2003 to November 2005 were White males aged between 16 and 25 years (All-Party Parliamentary Group Against Antisemitism, 2006b, p 53). The Greater Manchester Police submission also notably reported that *only four* of the recorded anti-Jewish incidents were committed by offenders connected with extremist organisations. Three of the incidents were linked to anti-Israel demonstrations and the other involved National Front literature delivered to the victim's home.

Admittedly, the police data only provide a very broad-brush picture of the profile of the perpetrators of anti-Jewish 'hate crime'. Nevertheless, they do appear to strongly indicate that although Black and Asian youths are over-represented among offenders in comparison with their representation in the population at large, it is highly unlikely that Muslim youths, or even radical Islamists for that matter, were responsible for the majority of incidents given that the majority of suspected offenders were White (White Muslims constituted only 12% of the Muslim population in England and Wales according to the 2001 Census; see Peach, 2006, p 632).

The qualitative data used in the *Hate crimes against London's Jews* study are somewhat more revealing (Iganski et al, 2005). In a typology of incidents inductively derived from an analysis of crime reports, four in 10 incidents appeared to involve the premeditated targeting of victims or property, premeditated in the sense that the offender engineered the encounter. In none of them, however, was there any explicit evidence that the offender was connected with an extremist group – although the absence of such evidence does not rule out such a possibility given that in general offenders do not purposefully leave behind evidence to identify themselves. Less than a quarter of these incidents involved face-to-face contact between the offender and the victim (Iganski et al, 2005, p 115, Table F1), and so the majority of the offenders were somewhat shy or timid bigots. In one case in which the offenders were not reticent about revealing themselves – according to the crime report – 'Arab-looking' suspects in a van called out to a Jewish man on the street, "Are you a Jew?". When the victim answered, "yes", the offenders jumped out of the van, and verbally abused and assaulted him. Despite this case, assaults on victims, serious or otherwise, constituted only a small proportion (just over one in seven) of the recorded incidents for the whole period 2001–04 (Iganski et al, 2005, pp 105-7, Table D1), consistent with the BCS evidence on racially motivated incidents as discussed in Chapter One.

Other incidents were clearly opportunistic in that they involved chance random encounters between offenders and subsequent victims, rather than being engineered by the perpetrators, and they begin to provide a flavour of everyday 'hate crime'. 'Opportunity is the root cause of crime', according to Felson, who argued that 'everyday life tempts and impairs potential offenders' (2002, p 35). In the anti-Jewish incidents in question it was a case of being in the right place at the right time for the offenders to vent their bigotry or hostility, and for the victim, a case of being 'in the wrong place at the wrong time' in the course of their everyday lives. One sixth of all the incidents fell into this category. There were no indications that the incidents were premeditated in any way. In one incident, according to the crime report, five 15-year-old boys who were playing football in a park were approached by a group of older youths who acted aggressively. One said, "Look at those Jews" and "Why are you picking up your bags? We're not going to nick anything, you f***ing Jewish c**t". Two of the victims were then punched and kicked. In none of the incidents of this type was there any circumstantial evidence in the crime reports to indicate that the offenders' actions were preplanned in any way. This is not to suggest, however, that the offenders did not make decisions that informed their subsequent actions. Felson suggests that 'offenders make *quick choices*' and 'these choices are not fully spontaneous. A decision made a split second before is still a decision' (2002, p 37, emphasis in original). Accordingly, 'Even without prior planning, an offender responds to *cues in the immediate setting* and decides what to do' (Felson, 2002, p 40, emphasis in original). A serious assault on a London street on a Friday evening against an Orthodox Jewish teenager which resulted in his hospitalisation clearly illustrates the instant decisions that can be made by offenders when the setting offers the opportunity. The *Jewish Chronicle* reported that the assailants, two White youths, were first witnessed by the victim attacking an Asian man. The Jewish victim reported: 'They were making monkey noises and slapping him on the head.... Then they saw me and said: "Now here's a Yiddo". Having just come back from Israel, I was on a high and told them: "I'm Jewish and proud of it". After that, they just went mad.... They started pushing me and spinning me around. They smashed my glasses and punched me on the nose. I could feel blood on my face and it ran on to my jumper. Then they got me on the ground and kept on kicking me in the head and neck. I didn't pass out but felt detached. I could hear them shouting: "You f***ing Jew; give me tuppence, Jew boy", the usual things' (Symons, 2002, pp 1, 3).

While these opportunistic incidents appear to be instigated *because of* anti-Jewish animus, whether or not that was the primary motivation for each offence was impossible to tell from the victims' accounts in the crime reports. But it was very clear, however, that some incidents arose for *other reasons* than anti-Jewish bigotry. In a number of incidents the offender and the victim first became embroiled in some kind of conflict and the situation then became aggravated with anti-Jewish animus. Parallels are clearly evident between such incidents and cases of interpersonal crimes more generally. Felson argues that 'most fights emerge from quarrels in which neither party is fully innocent.... Typically the police take the winner of the fight to jail and the loser to hospital' (Felson, 2002, p 24). Felson outlines an 'escalation sequence' in which 'one party perceives an insult from the other; he [sic] responds to the insult and escalates the confrontation; that answer evokes a similar escalation; someone throws the first punch, and so it goes' (2002, p 24). The anti-Jewish incidents in question were less dramatic and more one-sided in terms of culpability than the 'fights' typologised by Felson, but nevertheless they did display a similar pattern of escalation. The interaction between the soon-to-be-offenders and soon-to-be-victims started out as commonplace episodes in everyday life, but often ones in which offenders seemed to perceive that a wrong had been inflicted on them. In one incident a minicab driver asked a passenger to take his feet off the seat of the car. An argument then ensued which escalated to a point at which the driver pulled over and radioed the minicab office to ask for another driver to complete the journey. The passenger then grabbed at and repeatedly punched the driver, shouting, "I know your type, you're a f★★★ing Jew. You are the embodiment of everything that is bad about Jews in this country". In another case, a victim was verbally abused when he complained about a car blocking his exit from a car park. According to the crime report, 'The suspect was sitting in his car arguing with a female passenger. The suspect's car was stationary and blocking the road so the victim could not get by. The victim got out of his car and walked over to the suspect's car and asked the suspect to move his car. The suspect got out of his car … in a fighting stance position. He said to the victim "f★★★ing Jew, I'll spit on you", and "I'll get you"'.

Many incidents of this type, irrespective of whether the victim and offender had some prior acquaintance, will not be reported to the police, perhaps because they are seen by the victims as constituting part of the routine incivilities of everyday life. The following incident that occurred on a train journey, and was not reported to the police, was described by a witness, a Jewish person who was a passenger on the train:

> "The incident began as a more general incident but then developed an antisemitic flavour at the end. There was a young man, I would guess twenty-ish, who was making a general nuisance of himself, he had headphones on but he was playing his music very loud and disturbing a number of people in the carriage who all complained about it. He was with a friend and they were effing and blinding very loudly and several people spoke to them about that as well and they were quite abusive to everybody who spoke to them. But anyway, sitting in the row of seats in front of these two and directly opposite the aisle from me was a man who was wearing a yarmulke and he had a number of Hebrew books open on the table in front of him. When these two characters came to get off the train one of them shouted very loudly at this man who had been one of the people who had asked them to be quiet.… 'You're going to burn in hell Jew'. Then as they were leaving the carriage his friend, I guess, asked him what he'd said because he then repeated it. And he was laughing as if it was the funniest thing ever. That was it really, but it was quite unpleasant."

It is notable that in each of the incidents just described, the offenders seemed to perceive that a wrong had been inflicted on them by the victims, ranging from being asked to take feet off the seat of a cab, to moving a vehicle blocking an exit, and to being told to quieten down on a train. It is tempting at first thought to think that the animus voiced by the offender in such incidents is solely an emotional outburst, an expressive act, provoked by the wrong that they feel has been inflicted on them. However, in the time it took offenders to react, arguably a decision, a 'quick calculation', was still made about whether or not to react in a particular way. An emotional reaction is still a reaction based on a decision, even if taken in a split second (Felson, 2002, pp 44-50). It is possible that in the anti-Jewish incidents in question the offenders had taken the snap decision to restore justice as they saw it by inflicting a harm on the victim for the harm that they perceived had been inflicted on themselves.

Analyses of the problem of racist violence in the 1980s and 1990s touched on the national political climate that provides a context for acts of 'race-hate crime' (cf Gordon, 1986, pp 36-9; Smith, 1989; Bowling, 1998, pp 161-2). Perhaps not surprisingly, rather than examining the culpability of the state itself when focusing on the politics of 'hate crime', official analyses of the problem of racist violence have confined themselves to statements about the role of extreme right-wing groups in creating a climate for, and being implicated in, racist attacks. Such statements peppered the policy literature on racist violence across the 1980s and 1990s. It is potentially instructive therefore that over two thirds of the qualitative sample of incidents in the *Hate crimes against London's Jews* study (Iganski et al, 2005) corresponded with the period of the local elections held in London boroughs and elsewhere in England and Wales on 2 May 2002. Sixty-eight candidates from the extreme right British National Party (BNP) stood in the elections (Mellows-Facer and Young, 2002, p 22). Scholars and other commentators have observed that extreme right activity provides a climate in which 'hate crime' escalates (Hewitt, 2005, p 35). Notably, therefore, in relation to the occurrence of anti-Jewish incidents, there were no BNP candidates in the 2002 local elections in the four London boroughs, Barnet, Camden, Hackney and Westminster, that together accounted for the majority of anti-Jewish incidents recorded by the police. In other parts of London BNP candidates gained 22% of the vote in the Northend Ward of Bexley, 21.7% in Hainault in Redbridge and 17.4% in Downham in Lewisham. However, Redbridge is the only one of these three London boroughs that has a particular residential concentration of Jews (Graham, 2005, p 83). The absence of extreme right electoral activity and other activism in those areas of London that accounted for the highest proportions of anti-Jewish incidents appears to accord with the conclusions made by the recent All-Party Parliamentary Inquiry into Antisemitism about the threat of the far right to Jews. Although the Inquiry observed that '[d]uring the twentieth century the far right was the dominant source of antisemitism in the UK' and that it continues to articulate conspiracy theories about Jews, it concluded that although 'there is no room for complacency ... the overt threat from the far right may not be as significant as it once was' (All-Party Parliamentary Group Against Antisemitism, 2006a, pp 24-6). This is not to argue that politics was entirely absent from the anti-Jewish incidents recorded by the Metropolitan Police Service. Approximately 20% of the incidents in the qualitative sub-sample showed evidence of anti-Israeli sentiment in the discourse of offenders, and in some instances sentiment drawing on the Arab–Israeli conflict more broadly. But many of these incidents clearly crossed a line from anti-Israeli to anti-Jewish animus and in some cases anti-Israeli sentiment was accompanied by other abuse and racist bigotry. In one such incident, the victim parked his car outside an Asian restaurant. When he got out of the car to move aside a board on the footpath advertising the restaurant, the offender emerged from inside the restaurant and began swearing at the victim and said, "You're not in Israel now. You can't do what you like. Go back to Israel". The offender then continued to swear, and according to the crime report, shouted other racist abuse and kicked the car door, damaging it. This particular incident, judging from the circumstantial evidence, was not premeditated in any way and it indicates how the Israel–Palestine conflict triggers the venting of bigotry against Jews in general, as well as animus against Jewish people as Israelis in particular. The peak in incidents associated with raised tensions in the Israel–Palestine conflict therefore arguably reveals more the pervasiveness of anti-Jewish bigotry, than an outpouring of anger against the Israeli state. Events in the Israel–Palestine conflict clearly serve as a catalyst for the venting of that bigotry that simmers beneath the surface for many people.

In commenting on the prevailing social climate affecting Jewish people in France a few years ago, sociologist Pierre-André Taguieff proposed that 'Things have reached the point where we might reintroduce the old term "banalization". It is exactly as if many different attitudes and manifestations of Judeophobia had become banalized, as if they fitted so well into the ideological scenery that they were no longer perceptible' (Taguieff, 2004, p 3). Arguably, it is the banalisation of anti-Jewish sentiment that this chapter illuminates and that sentiment is made perceptible through the evidence of anti-Jewish incidents. When the situational contexts and the dynamics of incidents are unfolded, there is little apparent evidence that political extremism has been at work, despite what was the accepted wisdom about such incidents. This is not to argue that offenders affiliated with extremist groups have not been involved at all, or that individual Jewish people or Jewish communal property have not been targeted in premeditated attacks, as the evidence shows otherwise. But such incidents appear to be in the minority. Instead, the majority of incidents provide an indicator of the banality of 'antisemitism' in that they are not prompted by a particular ideological conviction or volition but instead in their expressive character they display a 'commonsense' 'antisemitism' that lies beneath the surface of everyday cognition for many individuals. It rises to the surface for some people when the opportunity to vent their simmering bigotry presents itself and it is often triggered by a grievance, an irritation, or conflict, things that are commonplace in everyday life but present a particular reflex opportunity when a Jewish person is involved. Arguably, this is no different from the occurrence of other incidents of so-called 'hate crime' to which this chapter now turns.

If we turn the analysis to anti-Muslim incidents that have occurred in an apparent backlash against the political outrages of the 9/11 terror attacks on the World Trade Center and the Pentagon in the US, and the July 2005 bombings in London, it is evident that there are clear parallels with the anti-Jewish incidents just discussed, in that many were seemingly committed by 'ordinary' people in the context of their 'everyday' lives, not by 'extremists' in the pursuit of ideological goals. Although published police data on anti-Muslim incidents in the UK following the 9/11 attacks are largely non-existent, there was clearly a backlash of bigotry manifest by ordinary people going about their everyday lives. The Commission on British Muslims and Islamophobia noted in its 2004 report that 'Thousands of British Muslims have tales to tell from the days after 9/11 – rudeness and insensitivity, or worse, from colleagues, associates and neighbours, and from total strangers in shops and buses, trains and streets' (2004, p 16). The Muslim Council of Britain received hundreds of offensive emails, most of which could be classified as malicious communications in terms of criminal law. And, judging from incidents recorded by the Forum Against Islamophobia and Racism, most involved either the deliberate targeting of visibly Muslim public locations, such as Mosques and cultural centres, or the opportunistic targeting of victims, particularly Muslim women made visible by their attire, a pattern consistent with the targets in peaks of anti-Jewish incidents that correspond with upsurges in the conflict in the Middle East (Iganski et al, 2005, pp 58-61).

To turn to more recent events, various claims were made about the occurrence of anti-Muslim incidents in the days and weeks following the bombings and attempted bombings in London in July 2005. In early August, BBC news reported that there had been a 'six-fold' increase in 'religious hate crimes, mostly against Muslims' (see 'Hate crimes soar after London Bombings', *BBC News*, news.bbc.co.uk/1/hi/england/london/4740015.stm). Similar claims about Muslim people being targeted in a wave of incidents were widely reported in the press. In the prevailing climate of violence against Muslim people Dr Zaki Badawi, head of the Muslim College in London, advised Muslim women to stop wearing the hijab, lest it mark them out for a beating (Appleton, 2005). There was, however, some uncertainty about the scale of the anti-Muslim backlash, as discussed in Appendix C to this book.

A small number of surveys indicated the prevailing climate for Muslim people shortly after the July 2005 bombings, and the findings are especially illuminating given the absence of published police data on incidents. For instance, in an online survey of 526 Muslim people carried out by YouGov between 15 and 22 July 2005, a week after the bombings, three quarters of the respondents felt that 'relations in Britain between Muslims and non-Muslims' had deteriorated since the events of 7 July. Fourteen per cent of respondents reported that they had been subjected to verbal abuse and 29% that members of their family or friends had been subject to verbal abuse since 7 July. Three per cent of respondents reported that they had been physically attacked, and 10% that members of their family or friends had been physically attacked since 7 July (see http://lewishamlistens.com/archives/pdf/TEL050101030_1.pdf). A few days later, in an ICM telephone poll of 500 Muslim people, 20% of respondents reported that they, or a member of their family, had experienced hostility or abuse from non-Muslims since the 7 July bombings (see http://image.guardian.co.uk/sys-files/Politics/documents/2005/07/26/Muslim-Poll.pdf).

A sample of incidents against Muslim people reported in the press is presented in Box 2.1. The sample cannot be regarded as representative in any way, especially, as noted in Chapter One, given that media reports focus on the most dramatic incidents. However, they do provide some of the flavour of part of the backlash on the streets. Most involved either the deliberate targeting of visibly Muslim public locations or the opportunistic targeting of Muslim people – again, consistent with the pattern of anti-Jewish incidents that corresponds with upsurges in the Middle East conflict. Where some detail about the characteristics of offenders was reported, many were seemingly committed by 'ordinary' people in the contexts of their 'everyday' lives: passers-by in the street, people out shopping, people driving their cars, colleagues at work and children at school.

Box 2.1: Sample of incidents against Muslims reported in the press following the London bombings in July 2005

7 July 2005. Dulwich, east London. **Pork dumped outside Mosque.** 'Worshippers at the Northcross Road Centre were also singled out on the day of the London bomb attacks when yobs dumped pork outside – a grave insult to Muslims. Haq, who led prayers for the London bomb victims, said, "We had just finished prayers for those who died when somebody spotted the pork". He described it as the work "of mindless idiots". Chairman of the Centre, Hussain Malik, said, "We utterly condemn the despicable attacks on London and we utterly condemn these criminal attacks on our mosque"'. (*The Muslim News*, 29 July 2005)

7 July 2005. **Arson.** 'Garage at the home of a Muslim woman in south London destroyed by suspected arson.' (Kirby, 2005)

7 July 2005. Fulham Road. **Pushing and verbal abuse.** A shopkeeper on the Fulham Road, west London, Aman Moradi, 45, is racially abused by David Parritt, a postman, who pushes her in the face before calling her a "f***ing Muslim". He is sentenced to 200 hours community service with £70 compensation and £85 costs after pleading guilty to racially aggravated common assault and racially aggravated criminal damage. (Judd et al, 2005)

9 July 2005. Bow, east London. **Islamophobi graffiti.** 'Graffiti was scribbled in a communal area in a private block of flats in Bow, east London on July 9. Metropolitan Police officer for Tower Hamlets, Superintendent Dal Babu, told *The Muslim News* that the perpetrators wrote on the walls, "Islam = death out now" and "Pakis out now". He said that the police washed the Islamophobic graffiti. He acknowledged that the graffiti was in response to the London bombings.' (*The Muslim News*, 29 July 2005)

9 July 2005. Mile End Road, east London. **Windows of Mosque smashed.** 'A place of prayer and learning for Muslims was vandalised within days of the London bombings. Every window of the Mazhirul Uloom centre on Mile End Road was smashed in the early hours of Saturday. It's believed those responsible were seeking to punish Muslims for the tube and bus attacks last Thursday. A reprisal against a popular educational and cultural centre for Muslims in London's east end.

Some in the local community have noticed attitudes towards them are changing for the worse.' (Channel 4 News, 12 July 2005: www.channel4.com/news/articles/society/religion/reprisal%20attacks%20against%20muslims/108855#fold_)

11 July 2005. '"Kill all Muslims" graffiti daubed on wall of primary school in Stratford, east London.' (Kirby, 2005)

12 July 2005. Hayes, west London. **Arson.** 'Asian family in Hayes, west London, victims of suspected arson attack when burning object is left outside home.' (Kirby, 2005)

16 July 2005. Dulwich. **Imam beaten unconscious.** 'Dulwich Islamic Centre's Imam became yet another victim of a vicious Islamophobic attack on Saturday July 16. The driver of a white van tailed Muhammed Haq as he cycled to Asr (late afternoon prayers) at about 7pm. The driver pulled over in Lordship Lane, Dulwich, south London, and repeatedly punched Haq shattering his cheekbone. Haq lost consciousness while the assailant fled. Despite the pain, the 27-year-old spoke of the attack. Speaking to *The Muslim News* Haq said, "I was on my bicycle when I noticed a white van beside me. It pulled over in the middle of the street and blocked my path. I assumed he wanted directions. He said nothing – but the next moment he was hitting me. He started screaming". Police quizzed a 20-year-old man on July 18, on suspicion of racist assault.' (*The Muslim News*, 29 July 2005)

23 July 2005. Central London. **Abuse and threats.** 'Muslim woman abused and threatened by National Front members during a march in central London.' (Kirby, 2005)

26 July 2005. **Attack with a baseball bat.** 'Man with a baseball bat attacked a car containing a group of women in Islamic dress in central London.' (Kirby, 2005)

29 July 2005. Sutton Common. **Attack in recreation ground.** 'Four Asian teenagers aged 16–19, are cornered in Sutton Common recreation ground by White youth who blamed them for the London bombings and then attacked them. One victim is left with a broken jaw, another needs six stitches to his lip and the others are bruised and cut after being punched and kicked.' (*Sutton Guardian*, 9 August 2005)

10 August 2005. Mile End. **Car driven at worshipper.** 'A worshipper at Al-Huda mosque in Mile End is nearly run over by a White man, outside the mosque, who drives his car straight at him.' (*Black Britain*, 11 August 2005)

The anti-Jewish and anti-Muslim incidents discussed so far are clearly not unique in character as they share some key commonalities with other forms of 'hate crime'. In the case of racist incidents, for instance, Ben Bowling proposed in his book *Violent racism* (1998) that manifestations of racism 'which lie on the border line of everyday understandings of "violence" – call it incivility, aggression, or threat – appear to be part and parcel of everyday life for ethnic minorities even in relatively affluent parts of central London' (1998, p 7). (Chapter Three of this book, which focuses on the spatial distribution of racist incidents in London, demonstrates that affluent areas are certainly not immune from the problem of racist violence.) While Bowling was writing about racist violence in London in the late 1980s and early 1990s, since then a number of research studies have provided empirical support to his assertions about the everyday dynamics of the problem. For instance, Rae Sibbitt's research on the perpetrators of racial violence in case studies of two London boroughs, commissioned and published by the Home Office (Sibbitt, 1997), offers qualitative descriptions of a panoply of everyday racist incidents that are strikingly similar to the anti-Jewish and anti-Muslim incidents discussed in this chapter. Similarly, Chahal and Julienne, in drawing from interviews and focus groups carried out in Belfast, Cardiff, Glasgow and London, observed that 'A depressing and regular feature of the project was interviewees expressing the "routine" nature of racism. Racism had become part of everyday experience in a variety of social situations, not just in and around the home but in shops, in the street and at school' (1999, p vi). Chahal and Julienne concluded that it was clear from their research that 'racist experiences are part of living for black and minority ethnic people and their white partners. This negative experience is seen as being part of the everyday structure of living – a routine, expected level of racism' (1999, p 37). The ubiquity of racist victimisation was demonstrated by a study of Glasgow commissioned by Strathclyde Police (Goodall et al, 2004), in which over half of the interview respondents reported that they had experienced several racist incidents in the last year and more than a third 'described incidents happening so frequently that they could not quantify the number involved'. Some of those victims reported that it occurred 'every day' or 'constantly'. The research also provides an indication of the ubiquity of offending as well as victimisation, for as Goodall and colleagues point out, 'The majority experienced this abuse from different perpetrators, rather than receiving repeat victimization from a single source. Over half of the perpetrators were children or "youths"' (Goodall et al, 2004, p 10, para 2.25). The presence of children and young people among offenders was also shown by a 'snapshot' analysis of the perpetrators of racist incidents recorded by the Metropolitan Police Service in 2001: 'one in four incidents involved locals, local youths and school children; one in five involved neighbours; one in ten involved customers; and one in 25 involved colleagues'; 'one in three incidents took place in/outside the victim's home' and 'three in ten incidents took place in work/school'. In addition, for the first six months of 2001 when 9,201 incidents were recorded, the peak time period for incidents to occur was between 3pm and 6pm, corresponding with the end of the school day, and perhaps not surprisingly during that time one in three of the suspects – in incidents where a suspect was known – was aged under 16, with under 21-year-olds accounting for 40% of all suspects (Metropolitan Police Service, 2002). The phenomenon of offending when schools empty their pupils out onto the surrounding streets is also evident for other offences in addition to racist incidents (cf Felson, 2002, pp 79-92).

To take a further turn in the analysis to focus on 'hate crime' against people with disabilities, the research evidence is limited compared with the evidence of racist victimisation and religiously motivated victimisation, but an accumulation of data from small-scale studies demonstrates some significant commonalities in respect of the everyday experience of the problem. For instance, completed questionnaires provided by 45 respondents in a recent study in London (Shamash and Hodgkins, 2007) revealed that almost a quarter of respondents reported experiencing 'bullying' because of their 'disability/impairment', with a similar proportion reporting 'name calling'. Nearly one fifth reported being 'harassed', almost one in 10 being 'hit, pushed, shoved, kicked or punched', with two respondents reporting 'being spat at'. One third of the incidents occurred on the street and four in 10 incidents occurred in other public places such as on public transport, at college, school or university. Tellingly, most of the respondents had experienced more than one incident and one fifth reported that incidents occurred 'all the time'. Almost half of the offenders were reported to be 'strangers', with over one half of all offenders reported to be children or youths and a further quarter of offenders reported to be 'young adults' (Shamash and Hodgkins, 2007, pp 25-7). The personal testimony of one of the authors of the report is very telling: 'To cite a personal example whilst undertaking one of the community research interviews at a voluntary organisation in Tower Hamlets, someone asked if they could speak to me about an issue. It transpired that they had been abused and pushed off a bus because of their disability. I left the building only for a young man to verbally abuse me in the most offensive manner, on the basis of me being a disabled person' (Shamash and Hodgkins, 2007, p 19).

The strong prevalence of victimisation was also revealed in research recently carried out by Mind, the National Association for Mental Health. Informed by a larger sample of 304 people with severe or long-term mental health problems living in the community who responded to a questionnaire survey, the research provides a disturbing picture of victimisation. In response to a question about crimes that had been experienced in the past two years 'related specifically to their mental health history', 62% reported 'verbal harassment' in taunting about their mental distress. The report notes that: 'respondents mentioned being called "psycho", "loony", "schizo", "nutter", "freak", "mad", "not all there", "round the bend", "thick", "stupid", "no brains", "wrong in the head", "obsessive". It was perpetrated in particular by young people, gangs or by neighbours' (Mind, 2007, p 6). The reported places of victimisation parallel the occurrence of anti-Jewish, anti-Muslim and racist incidents discussed above, taking place: 'on the street, in the local shop or on the bus. In a few cases, it extended into the school playground, where the children of a parent with mental health problems were bullied and made fun of by other children, sometimes encouraged or inspired by their own parents' behaviour'. Focus groups involving people with direct experience of mental distress and also support workers showed that the types of victimisation experienced were perceived by victims as 'hate crime'. And the research also noted the intersections between targeted identites of victims as some respondents reported 'being targeted not just because of their mental health, but also for racist or homophobic abuse or because they were transgender' (Mind, 2007, p 7). Just over a quarter of respondents reported that they had been sexually harassed.

These findings echo the research evidence from earlier reports. In a questionnaire survey carried out for the Disability Rights Commission and Capability Scotland, almost half of the 160 respondents with a disability reported 'being frightened or attacked because of their disability', and that it was 'part of their everyday lives' (Disability Rights Commission and Capability Scotland, 2004, p 13). People with mental health problems, learning difficulties and visual impairments were most likely to report attacks, with over half of the incidents occurring 'in the street, while out walking or in the park', and over a fifth on public transport (Disability Rights Commission and Capability Scotland, 2004, p 17). According to the victims, under 16-year-olds were responsible for almost half of the incidents, and they were most commonly a stranger or a group of strangers (Disability Rights Commission and Capability

Scotland, 2004, pp 19-20). (For further evidence about the problem of disability hate crime see: Mencap, 2000; Emerson et al, 2005, p 93; Respond, Voice UK and the Ann Craft Trust, 2007; Action for Blind People, 2008.)

To turn the analysis to homophobic incidents, four fifths (82%) of the 186 respondents in a 2001 survey in Northern Ireland reported that they had been victimised in some form of homophobic harassment, the most common being verbal insults, with over half (55%) reporting experiences of violence on account of their sexual orientation. Greater proportions of male respondents compared with females reported harassment and violence (Jarman and Tennant, 2003, p 38). The prevalence of victimisation reported in the survey appears to be higher than reported in other surveys, although it is not too dissimilar from reported victimisation of young gay males and lesbians in one of the earliest surveys of its kind in London (Stonewall, 1996). The majority of incidents occurred in public places – outside, or in the vicinity of an LGB (lesbian, gay or bisexual) bar or club, in the street elsewhere, sometimes near home or near work, and at school, college or university. Perpetrators were predominantly male with more than one perpetrator being involved in the majority of incidents of both harassment and violence. In over four fifths of incidents the offenders were reported to be youths or young adults, with 16- to 25-year-olds responsible for approximately half of incidents of both harassment and violence. Offenders were also known in some way to the victim in 43% of cases of harassment and 30% of cases of violence. They included people the offender had seen before, but did not know, local residents, work colleagues, fellow students, neighbours, and also, on occasion, friends and relatives (Jarman and Tennant, 2003, pp 37-55). A more recent survey carried out in Greenwich and Bexley in south London provides further evidence that in many incidents there is some sort of acquaintance between the offender and the victim, and in many cases even a family relationship. In almost two thirds of the incidents reported to have occurred in the 12 months prior to the survey, the victim said that they knew the offender (Moran et al, 2004, p 44), and in 28% of these incidents the offender was a family member, or ex-family member (Moran, 2007, p 85). One of the authors of the survey report, Les Moran, has more recently argued that '[m]ost of the homophobic violence taking place in London is routine violence that is occurring in the inner city and suburban homes, in the environs that surround those homes, in the workplace, schools and colleges of the metropolis. It is violence that is perpetrated by family, friends, neighbours, work-mates and colleagues' (Moran, 2007, p 92).

While the survey evidence just discussed shows that in many incidents offenders are 'known' by the victims, caution needs to be exercised in interpreting the actual nature of the relationship. Gail Mason has asked, for instance, whether an offender can 'be both familiar and a stranger at the same time?' (Mason, 2005, p 838). Just because victims might recognise offenders as being locals or someone else that they have seen before, and hence are not total strangers, it does not mean that they actually 'know' each other. As Mason points out, 'Victims tend to know suspects via their experience of the *location* of the incident. In other words, victim recognition of suspects is heavily dependent upon, or refracted through, the specific location or general vicinity within which the incident occurred' (2005, p 858). The significance of a shared experience of location as the basis of recognition between offenders and victims for the analysis of everyday 'hate crime' offered in this chapter is that shared use of locality provides the situational contexts in which everyday incidents occur, in the casting together of victims and offenders in the unfolding of their normal everyday lives.

Structure, action, agency and everyday 'hate crime'

For those who belong to communities victimised by 'hate crime' there is perhaps a sad and paradoxical comfort in the thought that offenders might be an aberration, confined to the margins of society in terms of the sentiments they express. It is somewhat more disturbing, however, to think that rather than being on the margins, they are among 'us', and many in the communities to which they belong share their sentiments. Those communities from which the perpetrators are drawn arguably share a collective responsibility for offenders' actions. Those who offend might be different from others in that they act on their attitudes whereas others do not. But offenders are not that different from others in terms of the particular values and attitudes that they share. Marcus Felson reminds us 'not to overstate the differences between active offenders and the rest of the population. The old cowboy movies had good guys (in white hats with white horses) and bad guys (in black hats with black horses). You don't have to be bad to do bad' (Felson, 2002, p 6). Such a reminder is highly pertinent to thinking about 'hate crime' offenders. In the case of racist incidents, for instance, Rae Sibbitt has suggested that there is a 'reciprocal relationship' between the racist attitudes of perpetrators and the wider communities from which offenders are drawn. According to Sibbitt, 'perpetrators see this as legitimising their actions. In turn, the wider community not only spawns such perpetrators, but fails to condemn them and actively reinforces their behaviour' (Sibbitt, 1997, p vii). Sibbitt therefore very aptly suggested that the wider community could be regarded as the 'perpetrator community' (1997, p 101) as there is in effect a 'critical, mutually supportive relationship between the individual perpetrator and the wider community' (1997, p 101). While the wider community shapes and legitimises the perpetrator's racism, the offender in turn serves the community 'in a vicarious fashion by taking their collective views to their logical conclusion and acting them out' (1997, p 101).

The pervasiveness of bigotry, and the collective culpability for incidents of 'hate crime', as suggested by the notion of 'perpetrator communities', provides a logic to the argument, as mentioned in Chapter One, that the label 'hate crime' wrongly individualises the problem as the abnormal, irrational and pathological behaviour of severely bigoted individuals. As mentioned in Chapter One, Barbara Perry prefers to use the term 'oppressive violence' to convey that 'hate crime' involves the exercise of power, which is entirely rational in the context of commonsense ideologies and discourses, or in Perry's words, 'deeply embedded notions of difference' (2001, p 46), about the communities historically targeted by 'hate crime'. These notions of difference serve to legitimise acts of 'hate crime' and from this perspective, 'hate crime' is an interactive process. By their actions 'hate crime' offenders are not only acting out these notions of difference, they are also at the same time reconstructing the prevailing structures of oppression and reinforcing the boundaries of difference. This process is made evident by the claims of some commentators that 'hate crimes' are 'message crimes'. The message conveyed by acts of 'hate crime' provides a reminder (McDevitt et al, 2002, p 308) – for victim and offender communities alike – of the victim's place. Therefore each act of 'hate crime' is another building block in the structural edifice of bigotry that in turn provides the context for offenders' actions.

The perspective that 'hate crime' offenders not only act out notions of difference, but that in doing so they also reproduce the structures of oppression that provide a basis for their actions, is characteristic of a core proposition of 'structuration theory', and conceptualised by Anthony Giddens as the 'duality of structure' whereby structure is conceived as both medium and outcome (cf Giddens, 1979, p 5; 1984, p 19). From the perspective of structuration theory structures are the medium of action providing 'stocks of knowledge' consisting of 'memory traces' and 'resources for action' from which people draw when they engage in social action (cf Giddens, 1984, pp 16-28). (This notion of structure contrasts with the orthodox sociological notion of structure as a patterning of social relations, embodied in the familiar terms 'class structure' and 'structural inequality', for instance, which conceive of structure in terms of the arrangement of material, economic and institutional resources, and systems of dominance derived from such arrangements.) In the case of the structures that provide a medium for action in instances of 'hate crime' we might think of the 'stocks of knowledge' as constituting a structural edifice of bigotry that provides a medium for offenders' actions.

In resonating the core of structuration theory, Perry has argued (2001, p 53), in the case of the structures that provide the medium for the actions of 'hate crime' offenders, that they are constituted and reconstituted by the actions of offenders, or, as Giddens proposed, 'the moment of the production of action is also one of reproduction in the contexts of the day-to-day enactment of social life' (1984, p 26). It is not the point of the analysis presented here to critically engage with stucturation theory, and there already exists an authoritative body of critical scholarship on the subject (for a review of the critiques of structuration theory, see Stones, 2005, pp 45-74). The intent instead is to develop further the propositions presented by Perry about the structural contextualisation of acts of 'hate crime'. However, because of the synergies between Perry's theoretical grounding of her analysis in 'structured action theory', as discussed in Chapter One, and the core elements of structuration theory, the aim here is to draw on some of the insights of structuration theory to inform a critical encounter with Perry's analysis. As argued in Chapter One, her analysis remains at the abstract level: while she argues that because of the symbiotic relationship involved, or the 'duality of structure', the 'structure–action' distinction is false, she does not go on to illuminate the chain of connection between structural context and the actions of 'hate crime' offenders. Without such a connection being made, an overly deterministic explanation is provided, which fails to account for the exercise of autonomy by individuals, and for why particular people offend in particular circumstances. It is this analytic gap that this chapter tries to fill. Clearly there are many occasions in which offenders engineer their encounters with victims in premeditated acts of 'hate crime'. But there are arguably many more occasions, as this chapter has tried to demonstrate, where the animus expressed by offenders, which lies beneath the surface of everyday cognition for many individuals, rises to the surface when the situational context provides the opportunity, or when it provides a trigger – perhaps a grievance, an irritation, a conflict, all events that are commonplace in everyday life.

Arguably, offenders in the types of incidents discussed in this chapter are not automata. As Giddens proposed, 'As social actors, all human beings are highly "learned" in respect of knowledge which they possess, and apply, in the production and reproduction of day-to-day social encounters' (1984, p 27). Therefore we might agree in part with Perry's proposition, as discussed in Chapter One, that 'hate crime' offenders are consciously and instrumentally 'doing difference'. However, her proposition that 'hate crime' is 'intended to marginalize' (Perry, 2001, p 214), and intended to sustain the social hierarchies which serve to legitimise victimisation (Perry, 2001, p 3), potentially attributes a degree of instrumentalism to the everyday ordinary offenders for consequences that they might not themselves intend. From an alternative perspective, the reproduction of hierarchies of oppression by acts of 'hate crime' might be regarded, to apply Giddens' words to the issue, as the 'unintended consequences of intentional conduct' (Giddens, 1984, p 12) on the part of offenders.

Conclusion: the significance of the situational dynamics of 'hate crime'

Very little research has systematically illuminated the connections between background structures of bigotry and the foreground of offenders' actions in cases of 'hate crime'. It is this missing link that this chapter has tried to provide by focusing on the situational dynamics of 'hate crime' in a shift in focus from the abstract to the empirical. It is in this spirit that the analysis offered in this chapter has tried to unravel the social circumstances of 'hate crime' offending, to not only attempt to understand better the situational contexts in which offences occur, but also to attempt to answer the pressing question of 'what brings some people to express their bigotry in acts against others?'. It was argued in Chapter One that to answer this question we need to begin with the social circumstances, the foreground, or the lived experiences, of 'hate crime'. What those experiences show when the situational dynamics of 'hate crime' are unfolded, is that contrary to the impression commonly conveyed by news reporting of incidents of 'hate crime', and also by some of the contributions to the scholarly literature on the matter, many offenders are not out-and-out bigots, hate-fuelled individuals who target their victims in premeditated violent attacks. Instead, many perpetrators of 'hate crime' are people like 'us', our friends, relatives, neighbours and work colleagues. Not only that, but many incidents are committed by such 'ordinary' people in the context of their ordinary 'everyday' lives. The prevalence of incidents of 'hate crime', combined with the ordinariness of offenders and offending, indicates that the sentiments that inform offending are intricately woven into the structural fabric of society and constitute a key component of 'common sense' (cf Gramsci, 1971, pp 419-23; Miles, 1989, p 70), which for many individuals lies below the surface of coherent cognition, but given the right circumstances, bursts to the surface. The ordinariness of many of the offenders is striking, and also extremely discomforting.

THREE

The spatial dynamics of everyday 'hate crime'

A key argument of the last chapter was that many incidents of 'hate crime' are not encounters engineered by offenders, but result from the normal frictions of day-to-day life. Or they take place when offenders seize an opportunity in chance encounters that occur in the course of the victims' and offenders' everyday lives. This chapter develops the analysis by demonstrating that the geography of space and place clearly plays a role in generating encounters between offenders and victims. It therefore mediates between the background structural context of 'hate crime' and the foreground of offending and victimisation. A number of hypotheses concerning the spatial dynamics of 'hate crime' are presented, drawn from the existing literature, and their salience for understanding 'hate crime' in the city is explored. Previously unpublished police data from London on 'race-hate' incidents are used to examine the geography of 'hate crime'. London was chosen as a case study as it is the most ethnically and culturally diverse city in the UK, one of the most diverse in Europe, and its rate of increase in diversity has outpaced the rest of the UK. Unfortunately, it is also the UK's capital of 'hate crime'. For these reasons it provides an instructive case study for analysing the spatial dynamics of 'hate crime'.

London: capital of diversity

To provide a context for the analysis that follows, the diversity of London's population and the problem of 'race-hate' crime in London are briefly outlined. The 2001 Census recorded more than 2 million London residents in Black and Asian minority ethnic communities out of a total population of 7.2 million. Among those who classified themselves as 'White' in the Census there were more than 220,000 Irish people, along with over half a million who ticked the 'Other White' group.

London is administratively and politically divided into 32 local authorities, or boroughs. According to the 1991 Census, the proportion of the population from Black and Asian minority ethnic groups was less than the proportion for all of England and Wales in only five of the

London boroughs. By the 2001 Census only three boroughs, Bexley, Bromley and Havering, had a smaller representation of Black and Asian communities in their population compared with the population for all of England and Wales. While the Black and Asian minority ethnic communities combined did not represent a numerical majority in any of the London boroughs according to the 1991 Census, by 2001 the boroughs of Newham and Brent recorded majority Black and Asian populations, with Tower Hamlets close to having such a majority. (The borough level data referred to in these paragraphs, and presented in Appendix D to this book, were extracted from a dataset kindly provided by the Greater London Authority and used in DMAG Briefing 2006/2; see Piggott, 2006.)

Given that it is possible that a growth in the numerical domination of the population in an area by one ethnic group can produce a decline in overall diversity, it is instructive to think beyond a White–Black and Asian minority ethnic dichotomy to examine ethnic group diversity more broadly. London was by far the most diverse region in the UK in 2001. Only two of the London boroughs in 2001, Bromley and Havering, were less diverse than the population of England and Wales. Each of the London boroughs increased in diversity between the 1991 and 2001 Censuses. Furthermore, each of the London boroughs, apart from three (Bexley, Havering and Wandsworth), had higher rates of increase in diversity compared with the rate of increase for the whole of England and Wales (see Appendix D). And in a 'diversity' ranking of English and Welsh electoral wards using the 2001 Census data, 12 of the top 15 most ethnically diverse wards were in London, a small increase on London's 11 wards in the top 15 most diverse in 1991 (Piggott, 2006, p 11).

Nearly 40% of Britain's Muslim population lives in the capital, along with more than half of Britain's Jewish and Hindu communities. From responses to the voluntary question on religion in the 2001 Census, about one person in 50, or 149,789, of London's population classified themselves as Jewish (Graham, 2005, p 83). London accounts for the largest and most diverse Muslim population in any city in the UK – the London boroughs account for 10 of the top 20 local authorities in the UK with the highest proportions of Muslim residents. Tower Hamlets has the highest population proportion (36%) of Muslim residents of all the London boroughs, and is also the third largest Muslim community in numerical terms. Tower Hamlets is also the centre of the Bangladeshi population in the UK, accounting for nearly a quarter of the Bangladeshi population as a whole (Peach, 2006, p 651).

London: capital of 'hate crime'

As headlined in the introduction to this chapter, London is also the UK's capital of 'hate crime'. According to police figures on racial incidents, London records the highest total number of incidents for any police force, accounting for just over one quarter of recorded incidents in England and Wales (see Table 3.1).

Table 3.1: Number of racial incidents recorded by the police (1996–2005): London* compared with the rest of England and Wales

	1996-97	1997-98	1998-99	1999-2000	2000-01	2001-02	2002-03	2003-04	2004-05
London	5,631	5,868	11,078	23,401	20,719	16,783	15,556	15,351	15,506
Rest of England and Wales	7,520	8,068	11,994	24,428	32,341	38,075	33,784	38,935	42,396

Note: * Numbers from the City of London Police and the Metropolitan Police Service combined.

Source: Home Office (2005, p 10); Home Office (2006, p 12)

Most notably, however, since the beginning of the current decade, the number of recorded incidents in London has fallen in contrast to the continuing rise elsewhere. In 2000/01 the Metropolitan Police Service and the City of London Police together recorded 39% of the total number of racial incidents recorded by police forces for all of England and Wales, a disproportionate figure given that London accounts for 14% of the population of England and Wales. By 2004/05 the number of racial incidents recorded by the police in London had fallen to 27% of the total for England and Wales. Given the well-known limitations of recorded crime statistics it is not possible to conclude from the police figures alone whether the data reveal an actual fall in racist victimisation in London. However, a decline in recorded incidents in almost each of the London boroughs apart from two, Bexley and Havering, does appear to suggest at first sight an actual decline in victimisation. Hammersmith and Fulham, Newham, Southwark and Wandsworth recorded a 50% fall in the number of racial incidents in 2005 compared with 2000 (see Figure 3.1).

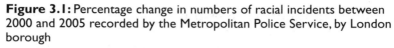

Figure 3.1: Percentage change in numbers of racial incidents between 2000 and 2005 recorded by the Metropolitan Police Service, by London borough

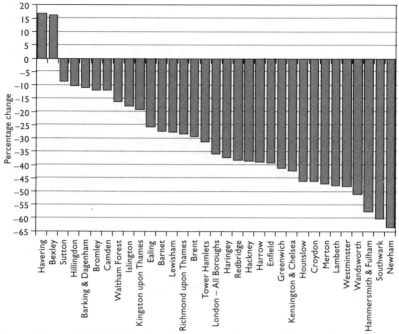

Source: Metropolitan Police Service. Freedom of information request No 2006040008701 PIB Crime/Performance Directorate for counts of incidents per borough per year

The analysis that follows uses data from the 1991 and 2001 Censuses of population focusing on the 'Asian', 'Black', 'Chinese' and 'White' groups, and data on recorded racial incidents for those groups for the calendar years 2000 and 2001 provided by the Metropolitan Police Service. Two years of police data are used because of their proximity to the 2001 Census, and also for comparative purposes to indicate whether there might be consistent patterns in victimisation across time. The ethnic group classifications used by the Metropolitan Police Service differ from those used in the ethnic group question in the 2001 Census. The category of 'Asian' is used in the analysis that follows for the police category of 'Indian/Pakistani'; 'Black' for the police category of 'African/Caribbean'; 'Chinese' for the police category of 'Chinese/Japanese'; and 'White' for the police category of 'White European'. Two remaining police ethnic group categories of 'Dark European' and 'Arabic/Egyptian' are excluded from the data used in the analysis due to difficulty in assigning these two groups to one of the other ethnic group categories, or to a classification used in the 2001 Census. A final police category of 'Unrecorded' is also excluded from the data in the analysis that follows.

An initial descriptive arrangement of the police data (see Table 3.2) reveals a number of patterns. As is the case for crime in general, 'race–hate crime' is not evenly distributed as shown by the incident rates for each group across the London boroughs. There is also an uneven distribution of victimisation rates between the groups, and the differences are substantial when the Asian and Black groups are compared with the Chinese and White groups. Despite that variation, however, the distribution of victimisation rates between the boroughs is largely consistent across the two years 2000 and 2001, indicating a definite pattern of victimisation over time.

In looking at the data in a little finer detail, the Asian group had the highest mean rate of victimisation, at 10.64 incidents per 1,000 population from the group in 2000 for all the boroughs combined, 10 times more than the mean rate of 1.05 incidents for the White group. The highest rate of victimisation for the Asian group occurred in the borough of Havering, at 27.75 incidents per 1,000 of the population in 2000, nearly 10 times higher than the highest rate for the White group that year at 2.99 incidents per 1,000 White population in Tower Hamlets. The rate for the Asian group in Havering was just slightly more than the neighbouring borough of Barking and Dagenham, which had the second highest rate for the group at 23.13 incidents. The mean rate for the Black group for the boroughs combined fell only slightly short of the mean rate for the Asian group at 9.23 incidents per 1,000 of the population.

However, the highest rate for the Black group in any borough fell considerably short of the highest rate for the Asian group. A rate of 21.9 incidents per 1,000 of the population was recorded for the Black group in Hounslow in 2001. Hounslow also had the highest borough rate the previous year. The Chinese group showed the lowest average rate overall, although in some boroughs, Barking and Dagenham and Bexley, in 2000 the rate was considerably higher than the White rate for those boroughs that year.

Table 3.2: Rates of racial incidents (per 1,000 population) recorded by the Metropolitan Police Service, by ethnic group and London borough (2000 and 2001)

	Incidents against Asians		Incidents against Blacks		Incidents against Chinese		Incidents against Whites	
	2000	2001	2000	2001	2000	2001	2000	2001
Barking & Dagenham	23.13	20.07	10.94	11.09	1.94	1.16	0.75	0.64
Barnet	5.71	5.69	8.64	4.84	0.08	0.11	0.88	0.67
Bexley	13.62	16.4	14.91	11.31	1.35	0.45	0.32	0.28
Brent	3.23	2.62	2.66	2.38	0.28	0.36	1.28	0.95
Bromley	12.41	11.44	7.85	9.03	0.56	0.50	0.31	0.30
Camden	8.3	5.41	8.62	6.96	0.20	0.32	0.81	0.93
Croydon	8.39	5.82	5.7	3.43	0.68	0.27	1.18	0.75
Ealing	3.45	3.12	5.16	5.51	0.33	0.06	0.78	0.53
Enfield	7.01	7.82	4.91	3.88	0.40	0.35	0.7	0.66
Greenwich	17.65	14.56	13.72	12.9	0.94	0.28	1.39	0.94
Hackney	6.21	6.21	2.83	3.02	0.42	0.25	1.94	1.93
Hammersmith & Fulham	16.44	11.3	10.26	7.74	0.84	0.23	1.39	0.85
Haringey	3.62	7.83	2.58	2.93	0.04	0.04	0.56	0.72
Harrow	3.69	3.3	4.56	5.92	0.08	0.16	0.97	0.91
Havering	27.75	28.79	12.88	11.69	0.45	1.47	0.24	0.18
Hillingdon	9.48	10.05	10.96	13.33	0.53	0.21	0.35	0.34
Hounslow	10.69	10.89	20.15	21.9	0.98	0.81	1.35	1.66

Table 3.2: *(continued)*

	Incidents against Asians		Incidents against Blacks		Incidents against Chinese		Incidents against Whites	
	2000	2001	2000	2001	2000	2001	2000	2001
Islington	12.7	14.96	8.76	10.56	0.16	0.39	0.88	1.22
Kensington & Chelsea	7.92	4.69	9.83	5.59	0.23	0.19	0.79	0.32
Kingston upon Thames	12.44	10.18	19.14	15.49	0.25	1.04	0.48	0.54
Lambeth	11.36	10.52	4.59	2.74	0.30	0.36	1.7	1.25
Lewisham	12.35	12.26	4.75	3.75	0.35	0.38	1.55	0.90
Merton	11.88	10.74	9.65	8.3	0.60	0.36	0.75	0.82
Newham	5.83	5.78	5.59	4.94	0.26	0.38	2.17	2.25
Redbridge	3.45	3.89	4.2	4.1	0.25	0.00	0.83	0.90
Richmond upon Thames	17.44	18.29	19.8	19.44	0.85	0.62	0.39	0.24
Southwark	15.23	14.88	7.77	7.67	0.49	0.22	1.97	1.63
Sutton	14.32	13.3	12.49	10.06	0.99	0.99	0.25	0.27
Tower Hamlets	4.89	3.69	10.8	9.74	0.31	0.17	2.99	3.93
Waltham Forest	5.24	5	4.65	3.17	0.35	0.28	0.85	0.89
Wandsworth	11.73	11.09	6.23	4.38	0.22	0.18	0.7	0.53
Westminster	13.05	10.03	19.79	16.12	0.47	0.39	2.02	1.31
Mean	10.64	10.02	9.23	8.25	0.51	0.41	1.05	0.95
Standard deviation	5.85	5.77	5.21	5.08	0.37	0.33	0.66	0.84
Median	11.03	10.16	8.63	7.32	0.40	0.34	0.84	0.74

Source: Metropolitan Police Service. Freedom of information request No 2006040008701 PIB Crime/Performance Directorate for counts of incidents per borough per year.

Inter-group friction and 'race-hate crime'

As stated in the introduction to this chapter, a number of hypotheses about the spatial dynamics of 'race-hate crime' can be distinguished in the extant literature. One of them, which might be called the 'inter-group friction' hypothesis, appears to directly accord with the conclusions drawn in the last chapter about the opportunistic and aggravated situational contexts of everyday 'hate crime'. The hypothesis posits that 'race-hate crime' is proportional to the amount of inter-group contact in a given locality. Higher levels of incidents relative to population size would be expected in ethnically heterogeneous areas compared with less diverse localities due to the increased opportunity for offending to occur, and the increased potential for inter-group conflicts to occur, because of the greater number of inter-group contacts in the course of people's everyday lives compared with more homogeneous areas.

The hypothesis can be explored by examining the association between two variables: ethnic group diversity in the London boroughs, and the rate of recorded incidents per unit of the total population in each borough. Figure 3.2, which plots the relationships, indicates only

Figure 3.2: Scatterplot of the association between ethnic group diversity in the London boroughs (2001) and the rate of 'race-hate crime' recorded by the Metropolitan Police Service (mean for 2000 and 2001)

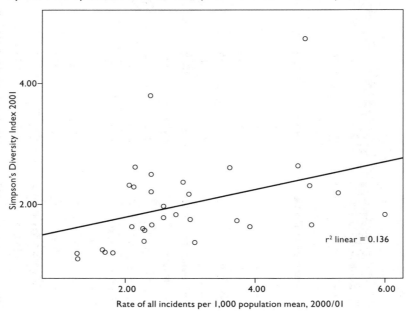

a weak association between ethnic group diversity and the rate of 'race-hate crime' in the boroughs.

A Spearman's rank correlation coefficient likewise indicates a weak association (0.447, significant at the 0.05 level [2-tailed]). There seems to be little support in the data from London, therefore, for the inter-group friction hypothesis. One reason for this might be that it assumes that 'race-hate crime' is an equal opportunities phenomenon, whereby the same potential for offending lies in each of the groups: the White communities and the minority ethnic communities. When this assumption is put aside, there does appear to be some support for the inter-group friction hypothesis, as the focus on power differentials, to which the analysis turns next, arguably demonstrates.

Power differentials and 'race-hate crime'

Another hypothesis, the 'power differential' hypothesis (Green et al, 1998, p 375), proposes that the rate of 'race-hate crime' against minority ethnic groups would be higher in those areas where minority communities account for a small proportion of the population. From their research in the US, Green and colleagues observed that 'Members of the dominant group may be emboldened to attack by the perception that law enforcement officials and the majority of those living in the neighborhood are unsympathetic to the victim group.... By the same token, where minorities are few in number, perpetrators have less to fear by way of reprisal' (Green et al, 1998, p 375). Research in the UK, focusing on the London borough of Newham, using a database of allegations of racial violence and harassment reported to the police by electoral ward between July 1996 and June 1997, and ethnic group population data by ward from the 1991 Census (Brimicombe et al, 2001), appear to confirm this hypothesis. The research found a strong positive correlation between the rate of alleged incidents against Black and Asian victims by ward and the proportion of the ward population that classified themselves as 'White' in the 1991 Census. Brimicombe and colleagues concluded that their results indicate that 'racial mix' in an area 'is an important factor in the rate of racially motivated violence and harassment', and they suggest that 'further analysis should be undertaken to explore this relationship for a wider geographical area' (Brimicombe et al, 2001, p 298). With this exhortation in mind, the analysis here examines the relationship between the ethnic group composition of the London boroughs, and rates of 'race-hate' incidents in each of the boroughs.

A preliminary analysis producing Spearman rank correlation coefficients (see Table 3.3) demonstrates a strong positive correlation for the Asian and Black groups for both years between the strength of the representation of the White population in the boroughs and the rate of 'race-hate' incidents against the groups, with a weaker association for the Chinese group. The correlation coefficients for the Asian and Black groups are comparable with the coefficients produced for the groups in Newham by Brimicombe and colleagues (2001, p 303). When compared with the inter-group friction hypothesis the difference that the correlation coefficients clearly indicates in the case of the London boroughs is that 'race-hate crime' is not an equal opportunities phenomenon, as the same propensity to offend does not apply to each of the groups and that it is the numerical dominance of the White community that is the important predictor variable for racial victimisation of minority ethnic communities.

But yet the very strong correlation coefficients for the White group create a conundrum for this conclusion, as will be discussed below. The data show that incidents against the White group are also very strongly inversely associated with the strength of the representation of the group in a borough: the smaller that representation, the greater the rate of offending against the group.

Table 3.3: Spearman rank correlation coefficients for rates of 'race-hate crime' (per 1,000 population), by ethnic group (2000 and 2001), and the White population percentage of the London boroughs, according to the 2001 Census

	2000	2001
Asian	0.715**	0.686**
Black	0.635**	0.566**
Chinese	0.424*	0.501**
White	−0.750**	−0.788**

Notes: * Correlation is significant at the 0.05 level (2-tailed).
** Correlation is significant at the 0.01 level (2-tailed).

The exploration of the power differential hypothesis to this point has, when focusing on the association between the strength of representation of the White group in a locality and 'race-hate' offending against minority ethnic groups, implicitly assumed that minority ethnic groups are only subject to 'race-hate crime' victimisation by the White group. However, there is evidence that inter-minority group offending does occur. Given the potential for such offending the exploration of the power differential hypothesis here shifts its focus from the power of the numerically dominant White group to the vulnerability of the numerically inferior minority ethnic groups by using for the independent variables the representation of the minority ethnic groups in the borough populations, rather than the representation of the White group. The dependent variables, the rates of incidents against the groups, remain unchanged. Such a shift in the focus of the analysis away from the strength of offender communities onto the vulnerability of victimised communities is consistent with the victim–centred approach to understanding 'hate crime' proposed in this book.

A preliminary analysis, again producing Spearman rank correlation coefficients, indicates a strong inverse association between the rate of incidents recorded for a group and the percentage of the group in the boroughs: in other words, the smaller the percentage of the total population that a group represents in a borough, the higher the rate of victimisation of the group (see Table 3.4).

To explore these evident associations further a least squares regression analysis was applied separately for each of the major ethnic groups: Asian, Black, Chinese and White. For each analysis the percentage of the borough population that classified themselves into the ethnic group in question in the 2001 Census was taken as the independent variable. The rate of racial incidents against the group per 1,000 of the group's

Table 3.4: Spearman rank correlation coefficients for rates of racial incidents, by ethnic group, and the population percentage of the group in the London boroughs (2000 and 2001)

	2000	2001
Asian	−0.758***	−0.804**
Black	−0.688**	−0.716**
Chinese	−0.520**	−0.335
White	−0.750**	−0.788**

Note: ** Correlation is significant at the 0.01 level (2-tailed).

population in the borough was taken as the dependent variable. Outlying residuals, beyond two standard deviations, were excluded from the analysis to minimise distortion of the regression models by outlying values where such distortion occurred.

For incidents against the Asian group in 2000 with two outliers included, Barking and Havering (both with higher rates than predicted by the model), as they did not distort the regression model, an inverse curve provided the best-fit regression line such that 60% (r^2= inverse 0.599, linear 0.424) of the variation in incidents could be explained by variation of the Asian population as a percentage of the total borough population. For the Asian group in 2001, a higher percentage of the variation in incidents (r^2= inverse 0.676, linear 0.420) could be explained by variation in the Asian population.

For incidents against the Black group in 2000, in excluding two outliers (Hounslow and Westminster, both with higher rates than predicted by the model), an inverse curve provided the best-fit regression line such that 62% (r^2= inverse 0.619, linear 0.459) of the

Figure 3.3: Regression analyses of the rate of racial incidents, by ethnic group (per 1,000 group population), recorded by the Metropolitan Police Service (2000), by the group percentage of the population in the London boroughs (2001 Census)

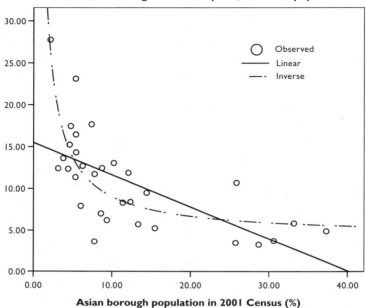

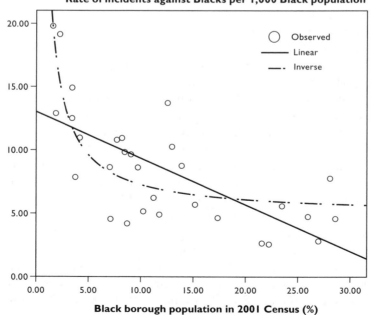

Figure 3.3: *(continued)*

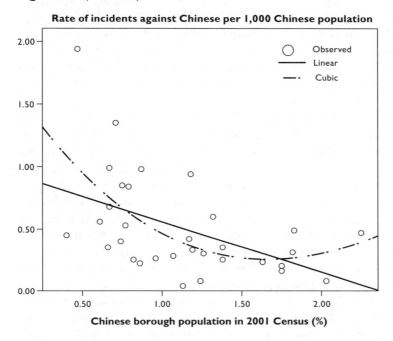

Rate of incidents against Chinese per 1,000 Chinese population

Chinese borough population in 2001 Census (%)

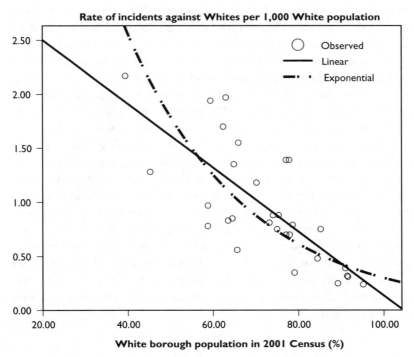

Rate of incidents against Whites per 1,000 White population

White borough population in 2001 Census (%)

variation in incidents could be explained by variation of the Black population as a percentage of the total borough population. For the Black group in 2001, contrary to the trend for the Asian group, a lower percentage of the variation in incidents (r^2= power 0.534, linear 0.410) could be explained by variation in the Black population, with a power curve providing the best-fit regression line and one outlier, Hounslow, excluded from the model.

For the Chinese group in 2000, with the outlier (Barking and Dagenham) included as it did not distort the regression model, a cubic curve provided the best-fit regression line but only to the extent that 33% (r^2=0.325, linear 0.234) of the variation in the rate of incidents against the group could be explained by variation in the Chinese population as a percentage of the total borough population. For the Chinese group in 2001, with two outliers included (Havering and Kingston upon Thames), a cubic curve again provided the best-fit regression line such that 48% (r^2=0.476, linear 0.261) of the variation in the rate of incidents against the group could be explained by variation in the Chinese borough population.

For the White group in 2000, with two outliers excluded (Tower Hamlets and Westminster, both with higher rates than predicted by the regression model), an exponential curve provided the best-fit regression line such that 60% (r^2= exponential 0.602) of the variation in the rate of incidents against the White group could be explained by variation of the White population as a percentage of the total borough population. For 2001, with the one outlier, Tower Hamlets, included as it does not distort the regression model, a slightly higher percentage, 63% (r^2= exponential 0.629), of the variation in incidents against the White group could be explained by variation in the White population (with an exponential curve providing the best-fit regression line).

What is notable is that for each of the minority ethnic groups included in the analysis (except for the Chinese group in 2001), there is a slightly stronger association between the representation of the group in the borough population and the rate of 'race-hate crime' against the group than there is when the strength of the White population is used as the independent variable (compare Tables 3.3 and 3.4). This suggests that while the strength of representation of the White group provides the dominant predictor variable for rates of victimisation of the minority ethnic groups, for any particular minority group the presence of other minority groups in the locality increases their rate of victimisation.

The geography of everyday 'hate crime'

The analysis of the spatial dynamics of 'hate crime' has to this point been somewhat removed from the spatial contexts of incidents as they occur in everyday life. To try to enhance the picture, it is instructive to zoom in the lens on London from looking at the boroughs as whole geographic units to smaller localities within the boroughs. Accordingly, the analysis here provides 'snapshots' of the geographic distribution of 'hate crime' within two boroughs, Lambeth and Barnet, using maps of incidents produced by the Metropolitan Police Service. The mapping of incidents, along with interpretations of the data provided by police crime analysts in the two boroughs, reinforces the observations made in Chapter Two about the situational dynamics of many incidents.

The main areas of concentration of reported 'hate crime' incidents in Lambeth in 2006, according to police records, were Brixton town centre and Streatham High Road. These are shopping and commercial areas with high rates of movement, volume and density of people

Figure 3.4: Lambeth 'race-hate crime' hotspots (2006)

and traffic relative to other localities in the borough such as housing estates. They consequently offer a greater frequency of contact and interaction, and therefore the potential for friction, between people in general, and between people from different ethnic communities, in various situations: in shops, on the streets and in traffic. Consequently, they provide a greater potential for everyday conflicts to occur which, as demonstrated in Chapter Two, in some instances become aggravated by racial hostility. They are sites of higher volumes of crime in general compared to other parts of the borough, especially street crime such as robbery, and they offer a greater potential for 'opportunistic' 'hate crime' offending by those so inclined. The 'hotspot' areas are also concentrated sites of the night-time economy of pubs, clubs and takeaway food outlets which provide a particular potential for conflict, and also opportunities for offending, when alcohol is combined with a mixture in flow and density of people.

There is a similar pattern of incidents in Barnet, and although two local authority housing estates, Grahame Park and Dollis Valley, experienced localised patterns of harassment of tenants, in general

Figure 3.5: Barnet race and faith 'hate crime' hotspots (2005)

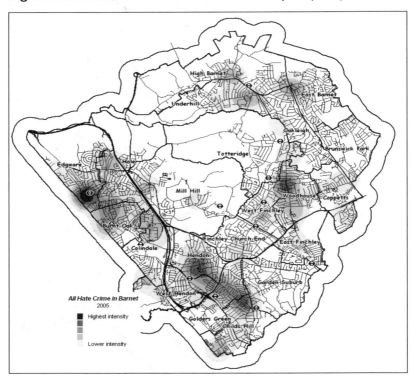

incidents were concentrated at spaces of higher everyday movement and density of people, particularly in and around the London underground stations and commercial shopping areas. While these two boroughs constitute only a small convenience sample, there are indications, from data presented by the London boroughs to the London-wide Race Hate Crime Forum (the work of the Forum in respect of victims of 'hate crime' is to be discussed in Chapter Five of this book), of similar patterns in the spatial distribution of incidents in other boroughs in London, although this would need to be verified by a far more extensive analysis than the snapshot provided here.

Defended neighbourhoods

Another dominant theme on the spatial dynamics of 'hate crime' evident in the literature might be coined as the 'defended neighbourhoods hypothesis' in that in some instances 'race–hate crime' can be regarded as an instrumentally defensive activity, defending neighbourhoods from unwelcome 'outsiders'. One of the early studies of the motivational dynamics of 'hate crime' offenders (Levin and McDevitt, 1993) identified a defensive logic at work on the part of some offenders (see also McDevitt et al, 2002) in their analysis of records of 'hate crimes' reported to the Boston US Police Department in the early 1990s. One quarter of the crimes were reportedly committed, from the offenders' prejudiced points of view, in order to protect their neighbourhood from those they considered to be 'outsiders or intruders'. The objective in some of these crimes, according to McDevitt and colleagues, 'was to convince the outsider to relocate elsewhere and also to send a message to other members of the victim's group that they too were not welcome in the neighbourhood' (2002, p 308). Such crimes might therefore be interpreted as an exclusionary process with segregationist objectives. Such territorial dynamics of exclusion are, according to Hesse and colleagues (1992), who focused on racial violence against minority ethnic communities and policy intervention in the London borough of Waltham Forest in the late 1970s and the 1980s, a manifestation of 'White territorialism'. From this perspective racist victimisation is an expression for the offenders of a sense of ownership, or propriety, to geographic space that they regard as 'White territory'. The presence and difference of the 'other', the 'outsider', is seen as a threat to the traditional spatial identity, or the 'ethnoscape', of the area. Hesse and colleagues argued that the significance of the notion of 'White territory' is 'evident in the connectedness of the victimization experiences' (Rai and Hesse, 1992, p 172). And from their perspective, acts of racial exclusion at the local level manifest wider exclusionary sentiment at the structural level in the face of perceived threats to the 'ethnoscape' of the nation.

Susan Smith has documented how such resistance evolved against 'outsiders' in post-Second World War Britain in a review of the literature (Smith, 1989). According to Smith, public opinion, as evidenced by opinion polls, shifted during the 1950s from 'relatively widespread indifference among white Britons to the presence of Black people' early on in the decade, to a growth in 'public anxiety' about immigration towards the end of the decade (1989, p 147). This shift in public opinion parallelled a shift in the attitudes of some politicians who voiced their concerns in Parliament. Smith concluded that by the 1980s 'popular consciousness had been infused with segregationist inclinations' (1989, p 150), and she also noted that in the 1982 British Social Attitudes Survey (Jowell and Airey, 1984) '40 per cent of the public associated racial strife with the location of "ethnically" mixed neighborhoods', and one half of the respondents believed that 'race riots' 'would be an enduring characteristic of Britain's urban future' (1989, p 148). In connecting the background structural political context to 'race–hate crime' and the values that fuel offenders' actions, Smith argued that the segregationist inclinations evident in public and political opinion provided 'a reservoir of procedural norms that not only tacitly inform routine activity, but are also available to legitimize more purposive, explicitly racist, practices' (1989, p 150).

The spatial arrangement of such 'explicitly racist' practices was noted early on in the 1981 Home Office study *Racial attacks* (Home Office, 1981), and also in the 1986 report of the House of Commons Home Affairs Committee (1986). The former observed that some local authorities reported that 'race–hate' incidents 'took place mainly on estates which were predominantly white. In many areas the ethnic minorities appeared to be concentrated on particular estates, and those in more outlying areas often sought to move back into estates with larger ethnic minority communities' (Home Office, 1981, p 25, para 59).

The analytic strategy followed to this point in the chapter has applied a static correlation of the rate of incidents against population composition by using just one point in time for the population data – the 2001 Census date. By contrast, earlier research using 'hate crime' data from the Bias Crime Unit in the New York Police Department for 1987-95 introduced population change into the model (Green at al, 1998). The introduction of such a dynamic element into the analysis is highly instructive for exploring the defended neighbourhoods hypothesis, as Green and colleagues showed an association between racially motivated crime and demographic change – there was an evident rise in 'race-hate' incidents when 'non-Whites' moved into traditionally White strongholds. The rate of increase of racially motivated incidents was positively correlated with the rate of 'non-White' migration into areas that were numerically traditionally White. Areas with larger and more established minority communities were observed to experience fewer incidents. The findings appear to support the defended neighbourhoods hypothesis that posits that 'race-hate crime' can in some localities be regarded as an instrumentally defensive activity, defending neighbourhoods from unwelcome 'outsiders'.

The data from London also appear to lend support to the notion of defended neighbourhoods. There was only a moderate correlation between the percentage change in the Black and Asian minority ethnic population in the boroughs between the 1991 and 2001 Censuses and the rates of incidents per 1,000 Black and minority ethnic population in 2001, with a slightly higher correlation coefficient than for incidents in 2000. However, a focus on the lowest quartile of boroughs, in terms of the percentage of the borough population that classified themselves into one of the Black and minority ethnic groups in the 1991 Census, is highly illuminating (see Table 3.5).

Table 3.5: Rates of racial incidents (per 1,000 Black and minority ethnic [BME] population, 2001), by percentage change in BME population proportion of selected London boroughs (1991–2001)

	% BME population in 1991 Census	% BME population in 2001 Census	% change in BME population 1991–2001	Rate of incidents per 1,000 BME population, 2001
Hillingdon	12.29	20.94	70.38	10.10
Kingston upon Thames	8.61	15.54	80.49	10.14
Barking & Dagenham	6.81	14.81	117.47	16.31
Sutton	5.91	10.80	82.74	11.69
Richmond upon Thames	5.48	9.02	64.60	15.24
Bexley	5.80	8.61	44.45	13.30
Bromley	4.67	8.41	80.09	9.53
Havering	3.19	4.83	51.41	22.63
Croydon	17.58	29.84	69.74	4.86
Redbridge	21.4	36.48	70.47	4.00
Harrow	26.2	41.23	57.37	3.95

Although there was clearly variation among the group, as a group these boroughs had a higher percentage change in the Black and minority ethnic population between the two Censuses than the rest of the London boroughs. In combination this group of boroughs also had a far higher rate of 'race-hate' incidents against minority ethnic communities than those few boroughs (Croydon, Harrow and Redbridge) that had comparable rates of increase in the minority ethnic population as a proportion of the borough population overall, but which had far higher Black and minority ethnic population proportions in 1991 compared with the lowest quartile group. This appears to support the findings produced by Green and colleagues for New York that showed an association between rises in 'race-hate crime' and the movement of Black and minority ethnic residents into traditionally 'White' strongholds.

The political economy of 'hate crime'

A variant of the defended neighbourhoods hypothesis adds the defence of material and economic resources within particular localities into the dynamics of defended space. Susan Smith argued that one manifestation of the segregationist inclinations in particular localities in Britain in the 1970s was support for the far right National Front party, and it was 'part of a white backlash against the local presence of a relatively large black minority' (1989, p 154) that occurred in declining industrial areas, where White and minority ethnic workers were brought into competition for jobs, and also in more prosperous areas, where there was competition for housing. Voting for the National Front was also disproportionately high in areas 'which themselves contained few black people, but which lay adjacent to districts in which the black population was statistically over-represented'. Smith argued that 'This suggests that racist voting is at least partly a reaction to the perceived threat of residential integration' (1989, p 154). Notably, in relation to the analysis offered in this chapter, Smith further observed that 'race-hate crime' mirrors this type of reaction as 'attacks tend to cluster in areas where black people form a small minority of the population, but appear to be challenging the territorial preferences of whites' (1989, p 161).

In this context, what might be called the political economy of 'hate crime' hypothesis has become a dominant theme in recent scholarly literature. Qualitative research in the UK, and also in the US, has reported a combination of spatial and economic conditions in the aetiology of 'race-hate crime'. For instance, Larry Ray, David Smith and Liz Wastell (2003) (see also Ray and Smith, 2002; Ray et al, 2004) drew out the motivations of 64 offenders in contact with the probation service in Greater Manchester, England. Half of their interview sample was unemployed, and those with jobs were generally in low-paid, low-skilled, casual or insecure work. Half had left school with no qualifications and half had convictions for other offences as well as non-racially motivated crimes. In this context Ray and colleagues argued that much of the violence was related to a sense of shame and failure, resentment and hostility felt by young men who 'are disadvantaged and marginalised economically and culturally, and thus deprived of the material basis for enacting a traditional conception of working-class masculinity'. Such emotions, apparently, 'readily lead to violence only in the case of young men (and occasionally for young women) for whom resorting to violence is a common approach to settling arguments and conflicts' (Ray et al, 2003, p 112). Ray and colleagues suggest that inclinations to such behaviour are widely shared among residents of disadvantaged neighbourhoods on the outskirts of Manchester. They reported that often the only contact offenders had with their victim's group was in commercial transactions, with shopkeepers and taxi drivers, for instance. In these interactions offenders were faced with people who were more economically successful, but perceived to be undeservedly so. Envy added to the emotional cocktail. Victims were scapegoated by offenders essentially looking for someone to blame for their situation. Ray and colleagues suggest that:

> Against a background of the routine, taken-for-granted racism that characterised their neighbourhoods, and in the context of a shared sense of being invisible and ignored, young men and more rarely young women for whom violence is an accessible and habitual cultural resource will readily identify those who are visibly different and visibly (or apparently) more successful as the causes of their shame and humiliation. (2003, p 125)

The socioeconomic context of 'race-hate crime' was earlier observed by Howard Pinderhughes (1993) from research with youths in New York City in 1990. Eleven focus groups were conducted with 88 youths attending a youth programme in southern Brooklyn working with White delinquents. The research revealed a combination of factors in the aetiology of 'race-hate crime'. The youths in the study were economically marginalised and frustrated, given limited job prospects in local and available labour markets. They perceived themselves to be victims of policy and practice that favoured minorities (an observation also made by Ray and colleagues): reverse discrimination and growing Black political power in the city. Living in economically disadvantaged neighbourhoods they saw themselves under siege and their attacks against the Black community and other 'outsiders' instrumentally constituted a mission to maintain the ethnoscape of their neighbourhood. The hostile and potentially dangerous reputation of the neighbourhoods was well known throughout the city, and served as a deterrent against members of minority communities visiting and settling in the areas.

Despite the persuasive qualitative evidence just discussed from the UK and the US, analysis of statistical 'hate crime' data for New York City by Green and colleagues did not reveal, in their words, 'a robust relationship' between 'hate crime' and economic conditions. They concluded that 'racially motivated crime emanates not from macroeconomic conditions but rather from threats to turf guarded by a homogeneous group' (1998, p 398). The weakness of socioeconomic correlates with rates of 'race-hate crime' was also indicated in the research by Brimicombe and colleagues (2001), in their statistical analysis of incidents recorded by the police in the London borough of Newham in 1996–97. Newham is one of the most disadvantaged boroughs in London and Brimicombe et al concluded that 'within an economically and socially disadvantaged borough these factors do not appear to account systematically for differences in victimization rates between groups' (2001, p 300).

Given the apparent contradictions in the findings from earlier research, the analysis here explores the relationship between socioeconomic deprivation and the incidence of racial victimisation across the London boroughs. An Index of Multiple Deprivation (IMD) is used as the independent variable with the rate of incidents for the minority ethnic groups combined used as the dependent variable. A preliminary scatterplot does not indicate a strong association, and any apparent association appears to be inversely related (see Figure 3.6). For instance, Tower Hamlets, which ranks 22nd among the boroughs in terms of rates of victimisation against the Black and minority ethnic groups combined, ranks highest on the IMD. By contrast, Richmond, which ranks the lowest on the IMD, ranks 5th highest in the rates of racist victimisation.

The relationship between deprivation and 'race-hate' victimisation is compounded by the distribution of deprivation across the London boroughs and the distribution of the minority ethnic communities, as represented in Figure 3.7. There is a strong positive association for the Black group between the extent of deprivation and the representation

Figure 3.6: Scatterplot of the association between the Index of Multiple Deprivation 2000 (IMD 2000) and the rate of incidents for the minority ethnic groups combined

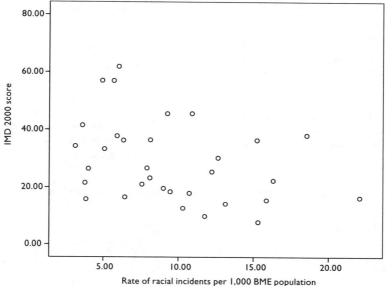

of the group in the boroughs, and weaker positive associations for the Asian and Chinese groups. As was shown above in the exploration of the power differential hypothesis, there was an inverse relationship between the strength of representation of the minority ethnic groups in the boroughs and rates of 'race–hate' victimisation against the groups. Given the positive associations between deprivation and the representation of the minority ethnic groups in the boroughs (Figure 3.7) we would expect an inverse relationship between deprivation and victimisation for the groups, as Figure 3.6 indicates.

Further exploration producing Spearman rank correlation coefficients to measure the strength of associations between selected indices of deprivation and the rates of incidents by ethnic group generated few strong associations and no uniform patterns, but some illuminating differences between the groups (see Table 3.6).

The strongest association between the indices of deprivation and rates of racial victimisation is evident for the White group in 2001, which is slightly stronger than the evident association for the group the previous year. To explore the association further a least squares regression analysis was carried out using the IMD (which combines each of the indices of multiple deprivation) as the independent variable and the

Figure 3.7: Distribution of ethnic groups across the London boroughs, by IMD

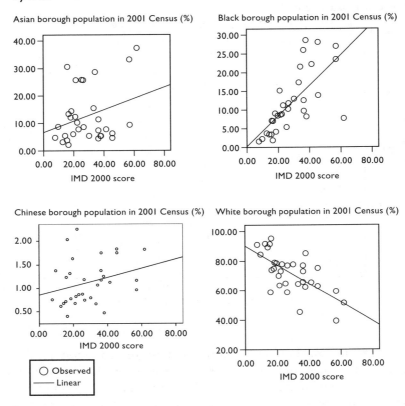

rate of incidents against the White group in 2001 as the dependent variable. With no outliers (beyond two standard deviations), a cubic curve provided the best-fit regression line such that 81% (r^2= cubic 0.812, linear 0.616) of the variation in the rate of incidents against the White group was associated with the variation in the IMD. This was a stronger association than the inverse relationship between the White percentage of borough population as the predictor variable and the rate of incidents against the White group as the dependent variable. This clearly seems to show that the smaller the representation of the White group as a proportion of a borough's population, and the greater the socioeconomic deprivation in a borough, the greater the rate of recorded 'race-hate' incidents against the White group.

Table 3.6: Spearman rank correlation coefficients for rates of racial incidents, by ethnic group, for the London boroughs (2000 and 2001), and selected IMD2000

	IMD2000	IMD2000 income score	IMD2000 employment score	IMD2000 education score	IMD2000 housing score	IMD2000 child poverty score
Asian 2000	−0.221	−0.210	−0.243	0.074	−0.385*	−0.175
Asian 2001	−0.152	−0.127	−0.179	0.194	−0.404*	−0.084
Black 2000	−0.413*	−0.424*	−0.461**	−0.200	−0.362*	−0.396*
Black 2001	−0.393	−0.400*	−0.451**	−0.220	−0.368*	−0.382*
White 2000	0.672**	0.649**	0.685**	0.486**	0.753**	0.647**
White 2001	0.740**	0.725**	0.741**	0.540**	0.766**	0.725**

Notes: * Significant at 0.05 level.
** Significant at 0.01 level.

Figure 3.8: Regression analysis of the rate of racial incidents against the White group (per 1,000 group population) recorded by the Metropolitan Police Service (2001), by London borough, by IMD score per borough

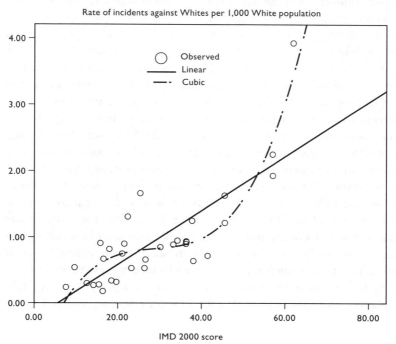

Rate of incidents against Whites per 1,000 White population

○ Observed
— Linear
—·— Cubic

IMD 2000 score

For the Asian group in 2001, even with one outlier excluded (Havering, which had a far higher rate of incidents than predicted by the model), a cubic curve provided the best-fit regression line such that only 32% (r^2= cubic 0.316, linear 0.023) of the variation in the rate of incidents against the Asian group was associated with the variation in the IMD. In the case of the Black group in 2001, with one outlier excluded (Hounslow, which had a far higher rate of incidents than predicted by the model), a cubic curve also provided the best-fit regression line, but only such that 38% (r^2= cubic 0.375, linear 0.135) of the variation in the rate of incidents against the Black group was associated with the IMD.

Conclusion: life in the city and everyday 'hate crime'

The data presented in this chapter show that 'race–hate' victimisation is not distributed evenly across the geography of London and greater rates of victimisation of minority ethnic communities are positively correlated with the numerical dominance of White communities and inversely correlated with the strength of representation of the different minority ethnic groups in the borough. Traditionally White strongholds that have experienced greater demographic change in terms of the growth in the proportion of residents from minority ethnic communities experience greater rates of 'race–hate' victimisation of those communities compared with areas that have experienced similar demographic change, but where the White population was already less numerically dominant. The earlier literature clearly shows how the struggle over material resources is an added ingredient in the cocktail of 'race–hate' victimisation. But the analysis presented in this chapter shows that there is not a strong, or uniform, pattern of association across London between socioeconomic deprivation and 'race–hate' victimisation. The data do, however, show strong correlations between the victimisation of White communities and the declining numerical dominance of those communities, and also an association between victimisation and socioeconomic deprivation in the case of White communities. But it is also clear that the rates of victimisation of the White group are far lower than the rates for the minority ethnic communities. A drawback to using a case study of one city for the analysis of a social problem such as 'hate crime' is that it opens itself up to criticism that 'it's not like that in New York', or Paris, or Sydney or in other diverse cities. It can be argued, however, that while the conceptualisation that this chapter offers is grounded in the experience of one city, London, it is not cemented to that particular urban environment and nowhere else.

The evaluation of the spatial distribution of 'race-hate crime' in London in this chapter arguably demonstrates how the geography of space and place mediates between the background structural contexts for acts of 'hate crime' and the foreground situational context of incidents. There has been a growing focus in the past decade and more on investigating, and drawing attention to, the experience of 'race-hate crime' rural settings, and small towns in rural areas (cf Jay, 1992; Dhalech, 1999; de Lima, 2001; Chakraborti and Garland, 2003). The earlier empirical research on 'race-hate crime' in the UK and other literature that this book draws on has focused on urban settings, but without consciously emphasising any distinctiveness of the 'urban' as a context for 'hate crime'. Arguably, the analysis presented in this chapter, and in the previous chapters, is self-consciously an urban analysis in which the processes involved are characteristic of life in the city. This is not to argue that everyday 'hate crime' does not occur in rural environments and small towns, because the research literature clearly demonstrates that it does. However, the density of populations, the volume of movement of people, concentrations of transport connections, shopping areas and the night-time economy of pubs, clubs and fast food outlets provide a distinctively urban phenomenon of potential opportunities for purposive victimisation and frictions that can become aggravated by expressions of bigotry. It was observed from the police mapping of incidents of 'race-hate crime' in Barnet and Lambeth that although there are patterns of targeting and repeat victimisation on some housing estates, the 'hotspots' for 'hate crime' were in those areas where people were thrown together in the melée of everyday urban life: areas in which everyday conflicts and routine incivilities occur, and areas which experience higher volumes of crime in general, not just 'hate crime'.

FOUR

Tensions in liberalism and the criminalisation of 'hate'

The 'New' Labour government elected in 1997 has often been criticised for the raft of legislation it has introduced and for its criminal justice reforms in particular. It might therefore be unfashionable to argue that under the leadership of Prime Minister Tony Blair the Labour government introduced a radical legislative programme against 'hate crime' that responded to, and was welcomed by, advocacy movements for historically victimised communities. In far less time than it took 'hate crime' laws to progress through state and federal legislatures in the US, between 1998 and 2003 provisions were enacted in the UK to provide harsher punishment for offenders whose offences were accompanied by manifest hostility towards their victims, on the basis of their 'race', religion, sexual orientation, or disability, compared with parallel offences without such accompanying hostility. To use the words of Derek McGhee from his book *Intolerant Britain?*, these provisions indicate an 'institutional and organisational reflexivity' that signifies a state which is becoming increasingly intolerant of intolerance (McGhee, 2005, pp 8–11).

At first sight, however, the punitive sanctions introduced by 'hate crime' laws might be viewed as being an exemplar of what David Garland has characterised as the decline of 'penal welfarism' and correctionalism in the US and the UK in the last three decades of the 20th century and the rise of punitive and expressive justice (Garland, 2001), whereby, according to Garland, there has been a replacement of the rehabilitative ideal fundamental to 'penal welfarism' by punitive measures that 'express public anger and resentment' about crime in both nations (Garland, 2001, p 9). 'Hate crime' laws might also be seen as being emblematic of what Ian Loader has similarly characterised as the fall (although not the complete defeat) of liberalism and the rise of 'penal excess' in the UK (Loader, 2007). But this chapter argues that some reflection on 'New' Labour's legislative initiatives against 'hate crime' suggests that they do not fit easily into such a depiction of penal policy.

The provision of equal concern and respect for all people, and respect for difference, principles that provide the motivating impetus for advocates of 'hate crime' laws, constitute a central plank of political liberalism. However, by criminalising 'hate', are illiberal means being used to achieve liberal ends? This chapter tries to grapple with this key question. Prior to 1980, in the US, only the state of Connecticut had established legal provisions against 'hate crime' that provide greater punishment compared with parallel crimes. Today, almost all states have such provisions. Throughout this period of time a debate has raged between legal scholars in the US, and it has also been played out by newspaper columnists in the country, about whether 'hate crime' laws are justified. Critics of the laws claim that they run counter to the liberal defence of rights to freedom of speech and expression, no matter how odious that speech might be, as words uttered by offenders are commonly used to determine their motivations. While the debate over the alleged clash of rights generated by 'hate crime' laws is now very well-worn, much ground still remains to be explored, and this chapter aims to offer some new perspectives to the debate.

How 'hate crimes' hurt more

Despite the comment made above about the justifiability of enhanced punishment for 'hate crime' offenders, a number of critics contend that such punishments are unjust as it is the offender's expressed values that attract the extra punishment. Such critics do not argue that 'hate crime' offenders should be immune from prosecution: rather, to the contrary, it is clear that they support the full weight of the law being brought down on offenders' actions. However, they argue that the additional punishment of 'hate crime' offenders over and above the punishment that can be meted out for a parallel, but otherwise motivated crime amounts to the state criminalising the expression of certain thoughts, opinions and values (cf Gey, 1997; Bruce, 2001; Hurd, 2001). They argue against such punishment in that in the context of a right to freedom of speech guaranteed by the First Amendment to the US Constitution (and by association the freedom of thought or opinion that lies behind speech), 'hate crime' laws contravene fundamental rights. Such rights are also incorporated into Articles 9 and 10 of the European Convention on Human Rights that is incorporated into UK law.

Such a concern about the conflict in rights has not been confined to debate in the US. Although the UK does not have such a written constitution, it has a long political and popular commitment to rights to freedom of expression, as the recent controversy over provisions against incitement to religious hatred, and the even more recent controversy over proposals to criminalise incitement to homophobic hatred, most starkly demonstrate. In this context of a commitment to rights to freedom of expression, columnist and social commentator Melanie Phillips argued that the provisions against racially aggravated offences in the 1998 Crime and Disorder Act were an 'Orwellian response to prejudice' (Phillips, 2002). More recently, columnist Johan Hari has argued, in the case of provisions criminalising homophobic incidents, that instead of providing equality of treatment for victims of such crimes, they provide special treatment:

> Hate crime laws undermine one of the most persuasive arguments of the gay rights movement. At every step of the way, all we have asked for is the same rights enjoyed by straight people: to have sex, to get married, to adopt. The anti-gay lobby has always claimed that we are asking for "special rights", and it has always been a lie. But hate crime laws do, finally, turn us into a special category. It says that stabbing me is worse than stabbing my heterosexual brother. (Hari, 2007)

Against such criticisms, supporters of 'hate crime' laws in the US argue that speech and other expression and the thought behind the crimes, or the offender's motivation, are not being punished (see Iganski, 2001), and that particular categories of victims are not being proffered special treatment. Instead, they propose that the laws impose greater punishment for the greater harms they believe are inflicted by 'hate crimes' (cf Weinstein, 1992; Lawrence, 1999; Levin, 1999). From this viewpoint, the nature and extent of the harm inflicted by an offence is critical for determining the appropriate punishment, and in the case of 'hate crime', the offender's motives are only relevant to determine whether the particular offence committed is a type of crime that inflicts greater harm than a similar, but otherwise motivated crime that causes lesser harm. From this perspective, the harsher punishment of 'hate crimes' simply provides the just deserts for the greater harm inflicted by such crimes. However, this argument hinges perilously on the evidence of the extent and type of harm inflicted.

Assertions that such harms occur have been evident in the policy literature and scholarly writing on racist violence in the UK for some decades, and were fundamental to the landmark case which settled the constitutional challenges against 'hate crime' legislation in the US – *Wisconsin v Mitchell* (113 S Ct at 2201 [1993]). There have been attempts elsewhere to critically unravel the evidence for these alleged harms (see Iganski, 2005), focusing on four different types of harm that might be distinguished: physical harm inflicted on individual victims; the spatial or terroristic effect of 'hate crimes' not only on the direct individual victims, but also the victim's community and other communities historically targeted by 'hate crimes'; psychological and emotional harms experienced by individual victims; and what might be referred to as a 'collective normative harm'.

Only a small minority of 'hate crimes' involve physical violence (as was shown in Chapter One in the case of racial incidents reported in the BCS). Therefore, even if the evidence was overwhelming that 'hate crime' victims suffer more serious physical injuries on average compared with parallel crimes (cf Levin and McDevitt, 1993; Levin, 1999, p 15) (which it is not), it would not justify greater punishment for all 'hate crimes' including those that do not result in physical injury.

A more compelling case for the harsher punishment of 'hate crimes' lies in the evidence of the spatial, or terroristic impact that such crimes can inflict on individuals and communities. Assertions about such impacts of 'hate crime' have been in evidence in the policy and scholarly literature on racist crime in the UK. For instance, the 1981 Home Office report *Racial attacks* drew attention to the role of the media in creating a climate of fear about racist attacks, arguing that:

> This is particularly true of reports in many local newspapers which appear to sensationalise apparently racial incidents. But it is also true nationally since, as close-knit communities, ethnic minorities are very conscious of what happens elsewhere in the country. Attacks on Asians in one place can cause great concern in Asian communities elsewhere. (Home Office, 1981, p 31, para 74)

The effect that racist attacks can have on a community were elaborated by Paul Gordon in the early scholarly literature on racist violence in the UK:

> Once attacks go beyond the isolated, the exceptional, they act as threat, an attack, not just against those individuals who are themselves the victims, but the whole group of people who consider themselves to be, who are at risk. In the same way that potentially all women are affected by rape or other violence against particular individual women, so all black people are affected by attacks on particular black people. When we speak of racist attacks, in other words, we are speaking of a form of violence against a group or a

community.... The reality behind these figures is a Britain in which, in some areas, black people will not venture out after dark. Where even during the day black people will take cabs to work or to the shops, where black schoolchildren have to be escorted to and from their schools. (Gordon, 1994, p 48)

Barnor Hesse and colleagues outlined the processes involved in the spatial consequence of racial attacks, drawing from their research in the London borough of Waltham Forest:

Asian and Black people form mental maps of the distribution of racial harassment ... people begin to perceive social spaces in "racially" particular ways. That is as locations which allow freedom of movement and those which inhibit; and locales which are "no go areas" or are relatively safe to live. In this sense the movements of people are shaped by the mental maps they "carry in their heads". Not only do settlement patterns illustrate this, but the functional use of space is also affected. The cumulative effect of these perceptions, based on real experiences, creates conditions where Asian and Black communities adjust themselves to being forced to live in and contest an unsafe social environment. (Rai and Hesse, 1992, p 177)

The impact on the spatial mobility of people from victimised communities can be considerable:

Their social behaviour may be restricted in the local environment because they have to live with not only ineffective responses from statutory agencies when reporting their experiences, but the reality of the harassment recurring. Several witnesses described these experiences as: "living under siege", encountering "total erosion of self confidence", finding themselves "turning into nervous wrecks", and having their capacity to live "normally" severely undermined. As a consequence the spatial mobility of people becomes restricted. Not only does this interfere with everyday life (eg going shopping, going to work, etc), it also restricts access to the use of public facilities. Some people felt unsafe using public parks. (Rai and Hesse, 1992, p 177)

Research carried out in Britain in the mid-1990s, the Fourth National Survey of Ethnic Minorities (Modood et al, 1997), demonstrated the wider behavioural impacts of 'race-hate crime'. Nearly one quarter of Black and Asian respondents in the survey said that they were worried about being 'racially harassed', and 14% of the respondents reported having taken measures to avoid potential harassment, in particular avoiding going out at night and other changes in leisure activity (Virdee, 1997, pp 284-5). It is useful to recall here that the enhanced penalties for offenders in cases of 'hate crime' are arguably only justified if greater harms are inflicted by such crimes compared with parallel crimes. Despite its compelling evidence, the Fourth National Survey of Ethnic Minorities did not provide a comparator group for such a conclusion to be drawn. (This type of limitation has affected other research on the harms of 'hate crime' as will be discussed below in the case of psychological harms.) Given this limitation, it is instructive to turn again to the BCS for some of the questions put to respondents who reported crimes (racially motivated and non-racially motivated) concerning their behavioural reactions following incidents.

It is notable that statistically significant higher proportions of minority ethnic and White victims of incidents believed to be racially motivated, compared with victims of non-racially motivated crimes, reported that they had "Started to avoid walking in/going to certain places", and higher proportions of victims of racially motivated crime reported having moved home (Table 4.1). The data are limited, however, with respect to evaluating the greater harms inflicted by 'hate crime'. As they concern the reactions of individual victims of crime they do not provide an indication of any wider behavioural impact, or the 'ripple-effect' of incidents beyond the initial victim. Furthermore, as the noted behavioural changes were reported by only a small minority of victims of racially motivated incidents, they undermine the justification for 'hate crime' laws on the basis of the greater harms inflicted, as almost half of respondents reported no behavioural 'harms'.

Much more compelling evidence of the greater harms inflicted by 'hate crime' compared with parallel crimes is apparent in the case of psychological and emotional harms. Assertions that such harms occur have also been evident in the policy literature on racist violence in the UK. For instance, the 1989 Home Office report *The response to racial attacks and harassment*, in making a case for multi-agency working, stated that:

> Take, for example, the family which is racially harassed by neighbours on a local authority housing estate. The mental

Table 4.1: Reported behavioural reactions following racially motivated and non-racially motivated crime (Column %)

	Minority ethnic groups		White groups	
	Racially motivated (%)	Non-racially motivated (%)	Racially motivated (%)	Non-racially motivated (%)
Types of actions taken after incidents				
Improved home security	5.6	10.7***	6.1	11.5***
Improved vehicle security	3.4	7.0***	0.7	5.7***
Started carrying personal security devices	2.0**	0.5	1.0	0.3
Started to avoid walking in/going to certain places	13.4***	2.6	15.3***	2.7
Started to avoid parking in certain places	5.5	6.8	3.4	6.0**
Moved house/flat	3.8**	1.6	5.4**	1.5
Changed jobs	1.1*	0.4	1.4	0.3
Tried to be more alert/not so trusting of people	17.3***	12.0	11.5**	8.2
Make sure valuables are always secure/locked away	2.7	13.4***	1.7	11.0***
No longer carry valuables/ money when going out	1.1	2.5***	0.7	1.4
Make sure valuables/ money are secure when going out	0.8	6.0***	1.0	4.2***
None of these	45.0*	41.0	45.1	41.0
Number of incidents (*n*)	655	5,607	295	39,368

Notes: The table uses data from variables TryPreA – TryPreP from the 2002/03 BCS, and TryPre2A – TryPre2R from the BCS 2003/04 and the BCS 2004/05. Data are for incidents that occurred in England and Wales and exclude incidents where respondents answered 'Other', 'Don't know' or declined to answer.
*$p<0.05$, **$p<0.01$, ***$p<0.001$

Source: BCS 2002/03, 2003/04 and 2004/05

and physical health of the family members may suffer; the children's physical and social development may be affected if they cannot be allowed outside to play; and older children may under-perform at school because of stress at home, or they may miss school altogether because their parents keep them at home or move house to avoid the problem.

Such a family may need support and practical help from the housing department, the police, community groups, the local tenants' association, the children's school, doctors and social workers. (Home Office, 1989, para 185)

In support of such observations, a substantial body of research evidence from the US has been published over the past two decades. The early research on the psychological and emotional impact of 'hate crimes' indicated the effects on individual victims, but due to the design of the research and the nature of the samples of respondents involved, the findings were equivocal on the question of whether 'hate crimes' hurt more than parallel crimes. For instance, in a small purposive sample of 'hate crime' victims Barnes and Ephross (1994) observed feelings of anger, fear, sadness, powerlessness, suspicion of others and bad feelings about themselves. But they also observed that 'to some extent the predominant emotional responses of hate violence victims appear similar to those of victims of other types of personal crime' (Barnes and Ephross, 1994, p 250). But in the absence of a comparison group for parallel crimes it was not possible to determine whether the psychological harms experienced by 'hate crime' victims in the sample were indeed the same or worse than victims of other crimes. The absence of a comparison group of victims of parallel crimes has affected the findings of subsequent research that further illuminated the emotional harms experienced by 'hate crime' victims (cf Hershberger and D'Augelli, 1995; Otis and Skinner, 1996). But more recently, Herek et al (1999) compared a purposive sample of lesbians and gay men who had been victims of 'hate crime' in the past five years (n=69) with a sample (n=100) who had been victimised on other grounds than their sexual orientation. They observed that the 'hate crime' victims recorded statistically significant higher scores on measures of depression, traumatic stress and anger. However, while their data revealed that *on average* victims of 'hate crimes' suffered more emotional harms, the evident variation in the scores indicated that not all victims experienced harm to the same extent, and potentially that some victims of parallel crimes suffered greater emotional harm than some victims of 'hate crimes'.

Arguably, one of the most comprehensive studies to date on the psychological harms of 'hate crime' was conducted by Jack McDevitt and colleagues (McDevitt et al, 2001), and involved a mail survey of a purposive sample of victims of assaults reported to the Boston US Police Department and victim advocacy agencies for 1992–97. The survey included victims of both 'hate crime' and parallel crimes. The survey questionnaire was designed to measure the psychological post-victimisation impact of 'intrusiveness' and 'avoidance' reactions according to Horowitz's Psychological Scale, utilising a 19-item scale. Six of the items presented statistically significant differences between victims of 'hate crime' and victims of parallel crimes, with the former reporting stronger reactions on measures of depression, nervousness, lack of concentration, unintentional thinking of the incident and thoughts of futility regarding their lives (McDevitt et al, 2001).

The research clearly demonstrated the psychologically intrusive nature of 'hate crime', and indicated victims' struggles post-victimisation. While the use of a control group of assault victims in parallel crimes was an advance on much of the earlier research, the design of the study had some limitations, as McDevitt and colleagues acknowledged. Chiefly, a low response rate to the mail survey and the purposive nature and the sources of the sample potentially introduced selection bias. In addition, given the observation in Chapter One of this book that assaults only account for a small minority of racially motivated incidents reported in the BCS, the range of victims in the Boston study was rather narrow. It is instructive therefore to return to the questions in the BCS on the matter. It was noted in Chapter One that for each of the major types of crime reported in the survey, higher proportions of victims who believed that incidents were racially motivated reported an 'emotional reaction' compared with victims of incidents that were not believed to be racially motivated (see Table 1.4), and the strength of the emotional reactions was consistently greater in racially motivated incidents (see Table 1.5). Additional variables in the survey further reveal the greater mental impacts of 'race-hate crime' compared with parallel crimes. Statistically significant higher proportions of victims in incidents that were believed to be racially motivated, compared with other crimes, reported feelings of 'shock', 'fear', 'depression', 'anxiety' and 'panic attacks', feelings of a 'loss of confidence' and 'feeling vulnerable', 'difficulty sleeping' and 'crying' (see Table 4.2).

It is notable that feelings of 'fear' manifest the highest differential in the types of emotional reactions reported. It is instructive to observe therefore that for each major category of crime, higher proportions of victims of racially motivated crime, compared with victims of non-racially motivated crime, reported being 'worried' or 'very worried' about future victimisation (see Table 4.3). (Fears about rape provide the only exception to the trend, as an equal proportion of minority ethnic respondents were worried about future victimisation, irrespective of whether or not they were victims of racially motivated crime.)

Table 4.2: Types of emotional reaction reported following racially motivated and non-racially motivated crime (Column %)

	Minority ethnic groups		White groups	
	Racially motivated (%)	Non-racially motivated (%)	Racially motivated (%)	Non-racially motivated (%)
Types of emotional reaction				
Anger	66.1	64.7	67.9**	62.9
Shock	46.4***	35.5	41.5***	24.2
Fear	38.9***	17.0	32.8***	12.0
Depression	20.7***	10.1	14.3***	6.3
Anxiety/panic attacks	16.8***	7.8	14.7***	6.1
Loss of confidence/ feeling vulnerable	32.9***	17.4	32.1***	14.5
Difficulty sleeping	19.2***	10.2	16.2***	8.6
Crying/tears	13.5***	8.4	12.8**	7.8
Annoyance	42.8	49.8***	49.4	58.6**
Number of incidents (n)	614	4,861	265	33,560

Notes: The table uses data from variables WhEmotA – WhEmotL. The data are for incidents in which respondents reported experiencing an emotional reaction. They exclude incidents where respondents answered 'Other', 'Don't know' or declined to answer.
*$p<0.05$, **$p<0.01$, ***$p<0.001$

Source: BCS 2002/03, 2003/04 and 2004/05

In the case of victims of non-racially motivated crime it is also notable that the same pattern applies: for each major crime type higher proportions of minority ethnic respondents reported worries about future victimisation compared with White respondents (see Table 4.3). The greatest differentials between minority ethnic and White victims, and between victims of racially motivated and non-racially motivated crime, are evident in the case of worry about physical attack, insults and racial attacks.

Table 4.3: Worries about future crime victimisation: a comparison of victims of racially motivated and non-racially motivated crime (Column %)

	Minority ethnic groups		White groups	
	Racially motivated (%)	Non-racially motivated (%)	Racially motivated (%)	Non-racially motivated (%)
Worry about...				
Burglary	69.7 (n^a=535)	65.4 (n=3,990)	62.1 (n=227)	55.4 (n=27,050)
Mugging	62.2 (n=535)	58.3 (n=3,983)	55.9 (n=227)	40.8 (n=27,022)
Car theft	66.8 (n=367)	64.5 (n=2,993)	63.3 (n=147)	54.8 (n=21,613)
Theft from car	69.5 (n=367)	66.2 (n=2,986)	59.2 (n=147)	53.9 (n=21,580)
Rape	41.6 (n=461)	41.6 (n=3,983)	38.0 (n=208)	27.1 (n=24,603)
Physical attack	69.9 (n=535)	56.1 (n=3,983)	55.5 (n=227)	40.6 (n=27,016)
Insult	69.3 (n=536)	49.1 (n=3,986)	49.8 (n=227)	34.4 (n=26,995)
Racial attack	71.6 (n=535)	43.3 (n=3,974)	43.1 (n=197)	11.0 (n=22,249)

Notes: [a] = number of respondents, not incidents as in Tables 4.1 and 4.2.

The table uses data from variables WBurgl, WMugged, WCarStol, WFromCar, WRaped, WAttack, WInsult and WRaceAtt. The data exclude incidents where respondents answered 'Don't know' or declined to answer.
*$p<0.05$, **$p<0.01$, ***$p<0.001$

Source: BCS 2002/03, 2003/04 and 2004/05

Punishing 'hate crime' offenders for their bad values

Could it be that it is the values expressed by offenders that account for the more severe psychological and emotional impacts of 'hate crime'? Frederick Lawrence, author of the book *Punishing hate* (1999), argued in a recent paper that victims of 'race-hate crime' experience attacks as a form of racial stigmatisation and that an incident 'carries with it the clear message that the target and his [sic] group are of marginal value' (Lawrence, 2006, p 3). The idea clearly proposed by Lawrence is that it is the message conveyed by the offender that inflicts the psychological and emotional damage: in short, it is the offender's expressed values that cause harm. From this perspective, the emotional harms experienced by a 'hate crime' victim arguably occur as a consequence of the victim's aversion to the attacker's animus towards their group identity. In essence, it is the attacker's values – painfully evident in their actions – striking at the core of the victim's identity, which hurt more. The assault on the core of a victim's identity arguably constitutes another common dimension of 'hate crime' when a victim-centred perspective is applied.

To turn the analysis here from the mental state of the individual victim to the collective conscience of society, Lawrence has also recently argued that 'hate crimes' 'violate not only society's general concern for the security of its members and their property but also the shared value of equality among its citizens and racial and religious harmony in a multicultural society' (Lawrence, 2006, p 3), and as Lawrence had earlier argued, 'hate crime' 'violates the equality principle, one of the most deeply held tenets in our legal system and our culture' (Lawrence, 1994, p 365). Given Lawrence's reasoning about 'hate crime' offending norms and values, and given the evidence about the mental impact of 'hate crime', it is difficult to do anything else but concur with the critics of 'hate crime' laws that they punish offenders for their expressed 'bad values'. That is what 'hate crime' laws do. But so does the rest of criminal law, as Kahan (2001) most cogently reasoned in his argument against the critics of 'hate crime' laws.

Criminal law in the UK is much more explicit in its intent to punish offenders' expressed values in cases of 'hate crime' than it is in the US. Jacobs and Potter argued that for an offender's actions to be labelled a 'hate crime' there must be a causal relationship between their 'prejudice' and their conduct (1998, p 21). However, such a rule would exclude the many incidents in the UK in which expressions of bigotry accompanying offenders' actions, but not necessarily impelling those actions, fall foul of the provisions for racially and religiously aggravated offences and for penalty enhancement where the offender demonstrates manifest hostility on the basis of the victim's sexual orientation or disability. The key criterion in each of these provisions is the demonstration of hostility by the offender at the time of committing an offence, or immediately before or immediately afterwards. In the case of racially and religiously aggravated offences the prosecution needs to prove the 'basic' offence, and then the racial or religious aggravation. On the matter of the manifest hostility, which is not defined in legislation, the Crown Prosecution Service (CPS, 2005) points out that for prosecution under section 28(a) of the 1998 Crime and Disorder Act such hostility can be 'totally unconnected with the "basic" offence' which may have been committed for other reasons. This was the case with a number of the incidents discussed in Chapter Two of this book where the incident initially occurred for reasons other than 'race-hate'. In the case of such incidents CPS guidance on prosecuting racially or religiously aggravated crime states that:

> Two cases decided by the Administrative Court illustrate the approach that courts have adopted when interpreting the law. In *DPP v McFarlane* (2002) EWHC Admin 485, Rose LJ found that once the 'basic' offence was proved (in this case a public order offence) and that racist language was used that was hostile or threatening to the victim, *it made no difference that the defendant may have had an additional reason for using the language*, the test under section 28(1)(a) was satisfied. In *DPP v Woods* (2002) EWHC 85 Admin, the defendant used racially abusive language to a doorman at a nightclub when expressing anger and frustration over being refused admittance. It was held, as in *McFarlane*, that the fact that the primary reason for the offence was other than a racist motivation the use of racist abuse during the commission of the basic offence made out the test for racial aggravation in section 28(1)(a). *The point was made that ordinarily, the use of racially (or religiously) insulting remarks would in the normal course of events be enough to establish a demonstration of hostility.* (CPS, 2005; emphasis added)

Compared with proving manifest hostility which may or may not be connected to the underlying offence, proving that such hostility motivated the offence is problematic, as recognised by the CPS, which asks: 'In the absence of a clear statement by the accused that his/her actions were motivated by his hostility to his victim based on his race or religious belief eg an admission under caution, how can motive be shown?'. The CPS suggests that it might be appropriate in some cases to use 'background' evidence to establish motive. Such evidence might be 'membership of or association with a racist group, or evidence of expressed racist views in the past might, dependent on the facts, be admissible in evidence'.

In sum, it is clear that the expressed values and sentiments of the offender play a key role in the imposition of harsher punishment under the UK's 'hate crime' provisions. This is especially so where the values that are expressed, that lead to the addition to the penalty imposed for the basic underlying offence, are not required to have anything to do with impelling that offence in the first place, or even at all. Furthermore, it is also possible that the offender's attitudes and sentiments expressed in the past, perhaps even expressed by their membership of a lawful but racist political group, can be used as evidence of their motivating state of mind in offences. Given these conditions under which 'hate' is criminalised in Britain, it is difficult to conclude anything other than that Britain's 'hate crime' provisions do outlaw the expression of particular attitudes, sentiments and opinions.

Everyday 'hate crime' and the declaratory value of 'hate crime' laws

Given the ubiquity and normality of everyday 'hate crime', as discussed in Chapter Two of this book, criminal law arguably provides an important symbolic cue against transgression by potential offenders. As noted in opening this chapter, the 'New' Labour government elected in 1997 has often been criticised for its criminal justice reforms. But they have included a radical legislative programme against 'hate crime', which responded to, and was welcomed by, advocacy movements for historically victimised communities. As also noted in opening this chapter, the punitive sanctions introduced by such provisions might be viewed at first sight as an exemplar of the apparent decline of 'penal welfarism' and correctionalism in the US and the UK, and the rise of punitive and expressive justice which manifests 'public anger and resentment' about crime in both countries (Garland, 2001, p 9). Such a concern has been shared by Ian Loader, who lamented what he saw as the demise of the contribution of the 'presumptuous paternalism' of criminal justice 'experts' to the management of crime in favour of a 'responsiveness to "consumer-citizens" which holds that the priority of the democratic polity' is to act 'as an uncritical cipher for, and translator of, the collective consumer will' (Loader, 2007, p 10). Jock Young has also contributed to what has now become the orthodoxy, that 'New' Labour's criminal justice initiatives have been a response to 'simple populism … a notion of giving the public what they want' (Young, 2003, p 36), with public opinion driven by the media clamour over crime (Young, 2003, p 41).

But some reflection on 'New' Labour's legislative initiatives against 'hate crime' arguably reveals that they do not accord with such a depiction of penal policy. As noted in the introduction to this chapter, the provision of equal concern and respect for all people, and respect for difference, principles that provide the motivating impetus for advocates of 'hate crime' laws, constitute a central plank of political liberalism. And against those who have argued that 'hate crime' laws use illiberal means to achieve liberal ends, the harsher punishment of 'hate crime' offenders compared with offenders of parallel crimes seems to be justified by the liberal principle of proportionate sentencing and provides offenders with their just deserts, given the growing strength of the evidence, as discussed in this chapter, that 'hate crimes' inflict greater harm than parallel crimes.

While 'hate crime' laws are clearly justified, the question to which the analysis now turns is whether they are in fact desirable. The argument offered here is that given the ubiquity of offending, the ordinariness of offenders, and the structural context for acts of 'hate crime' as outlined in this book, so-called 'hate crime' laws arguably provide a vitally important general deterrent against offending. They are not just targeted at the committed bigots who are potentially less likely to be swayed away from offending. They provide an important declaratory purpose aimed at the individuals who might offend in the unfolding context of their everyday lives, either when the opportunity prevents itself or a provocation occurs. And as von Hirsch and colleagues (1999, p 1) have concluded from their review of the research evidence and literature on the matter, 'there is by now unequivocal evidence that ordinary people can sometimes be deterred by both formal and informal sanctions.... To the question "does deterrence ever work?", our answer is that it clearly does'.

Barbara Perry has argued that 'hate-motivated violence can flourish only in an enabling environment' and in the US 'such an environment historically has been conditioned by the activity – and inactivity – of the state'. According to Perry, 'State practices, policy, and rhetoric often have provided the formal framework within which hate crime – as an informal mechanism of control – emerges' (2001, p 179). Perry has noted how in the US the state has contributed to the demonisation of Muslim communities in the 'war on terror' (Perry, 2003, p 193). The same point could be said about the state in Britain. The Commission on British Muslims and Islamophobia noted in 2004 that the targeting and disproportionate stops and searches of Muslim youths by the police, and the targeting and detention of Muslims under the 2001 Anti-terrorism Crime and Security Act, were not only contributing to the perception of Muslims as the 'enemy within' but were creating anger and alienation among young Muslims in particular (2004, pp 36-7). Such demonisation has become part of the edifice of the structural context for 'Islamaphobic' incidents in both the UK and the US.

However, if the state plays an important role in providing an environment in which 'hate crime' can flourish, the state can therefore also potentially play an important role in eroding that environment. Accordingly, the enactment of 'hate crime' laws in the

US since the 1970s, and in Britain the 'New' Labour government's radical legislative programme against 'hate crime', constitute a direct attack on the structural fabric that provides the context for acts of 'hate crime'. Through the imposition of a legislative regime of deterrence by the threat of the potential consequences of non-compliance (or, in other words, 'negative general prevention'), 'hate crime' laws are ultimately intended to reweave the structural fabric by setting a moral agenda (or, in other words, 'positive general prevention') for appropriate behaviour. The laws are targeted at the normative compliance of ordinary people going about their everyday lives – the situational contexts in which most 'hate crime' occurs, as argued in this book.

The establishment of this particular legislative regime in the US and in the UK does not appear to have been a case of pandering to populist sentiments, as implied by the orthodoxy lamenting the decline of penal welfarism. The lead appears to have come from the state, under pressure from rights-based advocacy, and not from any public clamour for punitive measures against 'hate crime' offenders. As also observed elsewhere (see Iganski, 1999), in drawing from an analysis of written responses to the 'New' Labour government's consultation paper on racially aggravated offences (Home Office, 1997), the provisions being proposed were supported by criminal justice agencies and by other agencies central to the era of penal welfarism that responded to the consultation exercise. A key expectation of the new legislation was that it would send an important message to agencies involved in the criminal justice system, providing the means and the impetus for a more effective response to incidents which would impact on the impressions of victim and offender communities about how seriously incidents were to be taken. In the case of the latter, deterrence is a subjective matter in that potential offenders will only be deterred if there is the danger of apprehension and they are aware of the penalties and the consequences.

The prevailing need for action by criminal justice agencies at the time the legislation was being proposed cannot be understated. Courts were not making full use of their powers of penalty enhancement in cases of racially motivated crime enabled by the 1991 Criminal Justice Act (sections 3(3) and 7(1)), or adequately following the lead provided in 1995 by the then Lord Chief Justice in *R v Ribbans, Duggan and Ridley* ([1995] 16 Cr App R[S] 698) for a proven racial element to be taken into account as an aggravating factor when sentencing. (Research for the CPS [1998] revealed that in only 22% of cases studied in 1997–98 where racial motivation was a factor, were sentences enhanced by the courts.) The provisions for racially aggravated offences established by the 1998 Crime and Disorder Act appear to have since had the intended effect on sentencing in magistrates' courts (although the impact on Crown Courts was more uncertain), as evidenced by research carried out on the first two years' use of the laws (Burney and Rose, 2002; Burney, 2003). Elizabeth Burney reported from the research that 'most opinion, from sentencers and other criminal justice practitioners, welcomed the legislation for its declaratory force and for providing clear structures and focus' (Burney, 2003, p 33).

In turning to policing, complaints from minority ethnic communities about the policing of racist incidents are long-standing and well known. Most significantly, the racist murder of Black teenager Stephen Lawrence by a gang of White youths at a bus stop in London in 1993 thrust the tragedy of violent racism, and the inadequacies of the police response to racist violence, onto the public consciousness in Britain with a potency perhaps never present before. The flawed police investigation into the murder, revealed by the Macpherson Inquiry (1999), became, for many, symbolic of the character of relations between the police and minority ethnic communities in Britain. Famously, using the language of 1960s Black Power activists in the US, the Inquiry report observed that the investigation was characterised by 'institutional racism'. Of course, the problem of the police response to, and handling of, racist violence and harassment was not first discovered by the Macpherson Inquiry, and the substance of the complaints about the police has differed little in the three decades and more in which they have been voiced. The 1981 Home Office study *Racial attacks*, for instance, indicated the lack of confidence and trust in the police that has inhibited the reporting of incidents by victims from minority ethnic communities. In revealing the belief that the police were in general unresponsive to incidents it reported complaints that the police failed to take action against known perpetrators, and, if they did take some action, 'no more than a word of warning not to repeat the offence' was given, and minority ethnic victims of incidents also complained of being arrested themselves by the police, or harassed by them after reporting incidents, especially cases of violence. The Home Office report observed that police forces 'accepted the need to take positive steps to secure the trust and cooperation of the ethnic minorities, and recognized that action to reassure the ethnic minorities about racial attacks was sensible preventive policing in light of the more serious conflicts which racial polarization would bring' (Home Office, 1981, pp 18-19, para 43). In an even-handed approach to voicing the complaints of minority ethnic communities and the response of the police, the Home Office report presented mitigating circumstances offered by the police that they claimed impeded effective investigation and detection of incidents, and, according to the report, the police considered that it was 'important the ethnic minorities should understand the limits which the law imposes on their ability to take summary action' (Home Office, 1981, p 19, para 44). Despite the claims of mitigation offered by the police, complaints of unresponsive policing of racist incidents have been echoed again and again by members of Black and Asian minority ethnic communities and well documented by empirical research (cf Virdee, 1997, p 279). An inquiry by the Greater London Council (GLC) Police Committee (GLC, 1984) revealed anecdotal evidence behind such complaints in a report not long after the publication of the 1981 Home Office report. The GLC report alleged that 'institutional racism' was prevalent within the Metropolitan Police Service, notably one-and-a-half decades before the same conclusion drawn by the Macpherson Inquiry. But the GLC report was particularly significant for pointing at London police officers as perpetrators of racial harassment. Complaints were made to the Inquiry about explicit harassment in the shape of verbal abuse and threats made to Black people by police officers in the course of stops and searches; the use of excessive and unnecessary force on Black suspects; and the abuse of Black bystanders and witnesses of crime; and Black victims of crime unconnected with racial violence and harassment were allegedly 'treated with suspicion, abused and occasionally assaulted' (GLC, 1984, p 11). There were complaints that Black bystanders and witnesses were abused or 'arrested for offences which arose during the course of an arrest of another person' (GLC, 1984, p 11). A more indirect form of harassment was reported in evidence that alleged that police chose 'to exercise their discretionary powers in ways which are arbitrary to the point of being unreasonable, unless racial bias is recognised as the motivation' (GLC, 1984, p 9). The GLC inquiry concluded that:'The result of these abuses is that London's police are viewed by many blacks with fear, suspicion and hostility. They are seen, not only as potential perpetrators of racial harassment, but also as sympathetic to the individuals and groups who continue to carry out harassment unchecked by the law' (GLC, 1984, p 18).

To return to more recent times and the Macpherson Inquiry report in 1999, from its evidential hearings in London and outside of the capital, the Inquiry reported that they 'were met with inescapable evidence which highlighted the lack of trust which exists between the police and the minority ethnic communities' and 'at every location there was a striking difference between the positive descriptions of policy initiatives by senior police officers, and the negative expressions of the minority communities, who clearly felt themselves to be discriminated against by the police and others' (Macpherson, 1999, para 45.6). The Inquiry report singled out the Metropolitan Police Service as being characterised by 'a greater degree of distrust between the police and the minority ethnic communities ... than elsewhere' (1999, para 45.23). And, reminiscent of the Home Office report *Racial attacks* nearly two decades earlier, the Macpherson Inquiry reported claims that the police failed to take complaints of incidents seriously, did not appreciate the impact of less serious 'non-crime' incidents, treated victims as the perpetrators of incidents, and furthermore, 'the "white" version of such incidents was all too readily accepted by police officers and others' (1999, para 45.11). In short, the Inquiry concluded that: 'Their collective experience was of senior officers adopting fine policies and using fine words, but of indifference on the ground at junior officer level. The actions or inactions of officers in relation to racist incidents were clearly a most potent factor in damaging public confidence in the Police Service' (1999, para 45.12).

Significant advances have since been made by the Metropolitan Police Service in the organisational arrangements for policing 'race-hate crime' and other forms of 'hate crime' in London, as described by Nathan Hall (2005, pp 168-89). Hall argues, for instance, that the challenge of policing diversity in London 'was recognized at the highest level and the MPS [Metropolitan Police Service] acknowledged that significant changes needed to be made to their operational approach in terms of defining standards for investigations, training, senior management oversight and the demonstration of fair practice' (Hall, 2005, pp 171-2).

It is difficult to discern from the scholarly literature alone the extent to which the provisions for racially aggravated offences established by the 1998 Crime and Disorder Act have provided a policy impetus for the Metropolitan Police Service. The impact of the provisions is not mentioned by Hall, who draws attention instead to the impact of the criticism levelled at the Metropolitan Police Service by the Macpherson Inquiry and by the ministerial priority recommended by the Inquiry report for all police forces to: 'increase trust and confidence in policing amongst minority ethnic communities' (Macpherson, 1999, p 27). What is clear is that very similar complaints to those just discussed about the policing of 'race-hate crime' over a number of decades have more recently been raised about the policing of other victims of 'hate crime', underlining the need for a continuing impetus on criminal justice agencies to intervene more effectively. To take some of the most recent complaints, Mind's report on its research carried out on 'hate crime' against people with mental health difficulties, discussed in

Chapter Two of this book, noted that 'people with mental distress are not taken seriously or simply not believed' (Mind, 2007, p 15) when it comes to the reporting of 'hate crime'. Just over a third of victims decided not to report incidents to the police for this reason; just over a quarter believed that they would not be seen as a priority; and just under a quarter did not think that anything would be done (Mind, 2007, p 9). When incidents were reported to the police, according to Mind, 'Respondents told us they felt visible signs of emotional distress had influenced police officers to think the victim was overreacting to a trivial incident' (Mind, 2007, p 15). The consequence of such a response was that 'Sixty per cent of respondents who reported a crime felt that the appropriate authority did not take the incident seriously' (Mind, 2007, p 15). Given such evidence it is difficult to reach any other conclusion than that victims are being re-victimised by the very agencies that should be expected to support them. (This, of course, has applied in the case of the policing of 'race-hate' incidents as discussed above.) As the Mind report notes, some respondents 'felt guilty for what had happened and blamed themselves. This was often the case when the police showed a lack of interest in their version of events. Respondents felt they must be overreacting since no-one saw their experience as a priority' (Mind, 2007, p 10).

Conclusion: legislating morality

In a critique of the argument that the provisions for racially aggravated offences established by the 1998 Crime and Disorder Act have provided an important impetus for the criminal justice system, Bill Dixon and David Gadd (2006) have recently argued that even if the provisions have 'encouraged the police and the rest of the justice system to take racially aggravated offending (more) seriously, it is hard to justify using the criminal law to send a hortatory message to institutions and individuals that have been charged with enforcing it but, by implication, are failing to do so' (p 316). In referring to the biographical details of some of their small sample of 15 people 'convicted of, or implicated in, some form of racially motivated violence or harassment' (Dixon and Gadd, 2006, p 315) included in the research, the prime reason offered is that the impetus 'operates only by further criminalizing people who are already seriously disadvantaged in a number of ways, not least by virtue of their previous contacts with the criminal justice system' (2006, p 316), and that the provisions for racially aggravated offences 'may be used against (often multiply) disadvantaged people, including individuals from minority ethnic backgrounds' (2006, p 317). This perspective sits firmly in the interventionist rehabilitative ethos of penal welfarism as the social and mental health needs of the offenders in question clearly indicate that welfarist, rather than punitive, interventions are more appropriate as punitive sanctions will only compound the serious difficulties that such people are experiencing. As it provides an important objection to penalty enhancement for offences that are aggravated by expressed bigotry it is instructive to engage with it point-by-point. First, it would clearly be unreasonable if unjust means were used to spur the criminal justice system into action. However, such injustice does not occur. The growing body of evidence on the harms inflicted by 'hate crime' as discussed arguably indicates that the harsher punishment of offences aggravated by hostility on the basis of the victim's 'race', religion, sexual orientation or disability, compared with similar crimes without such aggravation, pursues the liberal principle of proportionate sentencing and provides offenders with their just deserts. In theory it also potentially provides more equitable treatment to offenders by ensuring a greater level of fairness and consistency in sentencing than when penalty enhancement is left to the discretion of the courts (Cohen, 1999, p 111). However, even though the harsher punishment of 'hate crime' offenders is justified, it may not be desirable in some instances. The compounding of disadvantage on already disadvantaged offenders provides a serious point of concern. Although the evidence about the extent to which 'hate crime' offending is committed by individuals with psycho-social problems, such as drug and alcohol abuse and mental health difficulties, is presently very thin, and in obvious need of further research, there is clearly a case for flexibility and alternative interventionist measures for such offenders, rather than punishment. Given the extent of offending, however, such perpetrators are likely to be only a small minority of those responsible (on this point see also Hemmerman et al, 2007, p 11) and the punitive deterrence of so-called 'hate crime' laws is targeted at the majority of very ordinary offenders and the value systems that provide the contexts for their actions. It is the persistence and the ubiquity of those value systems, made visible by the prevalence of 'hate crime', that underpins the desirability of 'hate crime' laws, not only to prompt criminal justice agents to respond appropriately to victims, but more significantly to serve as a cue against potential transgression.

The suggestion has been made, in the case of provisions for racially aggravated offences, that prosecution should be 'mainly reserved for more serious or recalcitrant cases' (Burney and Rose, 2002, p 116) for fear in part of stoking resentment among those accused of 'minor incidents'. From their evaluation of the first two years' use of the provisions against racially aggravated offences, Burney and Rose observed that 'most people accused of a racially aggravated offence vehemently deny the accusation not merely because they fear a heavier penalty but because they recognise the shame of a racist label' (2002, p 115). The conclusion consequently drawn by Burney and Rose was that 'This surely demonstrates that the law is on the side of public opinion, not against it. But if it is misused, or too much attention paid to very minor incidents simply in order to get a "result", public opinion may change' (2002, p 115). It is important to recall, however, as discussed in Chapter One in the case of the emotional harms inflicted by 'race-hate crime', that so-called 'minor' offences can produce as much harm for victims as so-called 'serious' offences (see Tables 1.4 and 1.5). Furthermore, while flexibility in the application of the law is clearly important, as discussed above, and while alternatives to prosecution will be acceptable to many individual victims of 'hate crime', it is important to also recall that the individual victim is only the 'initial' victim as the impact of incidents extends well beyond the person targeted to others who are terrorised by incidents. And even more widely, at the societal level, 'hate crime' offends against particular dominant norms and values, in particular, the 'equality principle', to use the words of Fred Lawrence as discussed above, and a commitment to, and respect for, diversity (although such norms are not universally shared, as the prevalence of 'hate crime' most starkly demonstrates). Each individual act of 'hate crime' therefore has many victims.

In this context it is instructive to consider that the reach of the law is intended to extend well beyond individual perpetrators and individual victims. Despite Burney and Rose's assertion about the provisions against racially aggravated offences being in tune with public opinion, arguably the prevalence of 'hate crime' illuminates a more fractured and malign collective sentiment. As discussed in Chapter Two, individual offenders serve as proxies for the sentiments and values shared by many in the communities to which they belong. 'Hate crime' laws are thus targeted at the collective conscience, as well as the individual offender, in an explicit attempt to legislate morality. That is why 'New' Labour's legislative programme against 'hate crime' has been a radical intervention: rather than pandering to public sentiment for the imposition of punitive justice, it has been designed to promote justice by attempting to mould the collective conscience.

FIVE

Including victims of 'hate crime' in the criminal justice policy process

There seems to be a consensus in contemporary scholarly writing on victims of crime in the UK that they had first been 'lost', but then 'rediscovered' by criminal justice (cf Sanders, 2002, p 200). For some commentators, recent policy initiatives represent a 'watershed', with the interests of victims now nearing the top of the political agenda (Reeves and Mulley, 2000, pp 125, 144). A number of initiatives have been introduced from the 1960s onwards to make criminal justice more inclusive of victims, once the 'forgotten actors' of the criminal justice system (Sanders, 2002, p 200). This initial neglect of victims up until the late 1970s was mirrored by neglect on the part of criminologists (Rock, 2002, p 1); but a concern with victims now constitutes a major focus of academic criminology. However, criminologists' perspectives on measures to make the criminal justice process more inclusive for victims have been far from positive. Joanna Shapland has argued, for instance, that after over three decades of policy initiatives, 'there is little idea that victims are fundamentally woven into justice – that justice incorporates both victims and offenders', and scrutiny of the difficulties that victims continue to face indicate the 'need for criminal justice agencies to reach out and respond to victims' (Shapland, 2000, p 148). Some commentators who believe that there has been a 'shift in culture' in criminal justice, and that the initiatives for victims are a 'cause for celebration', have also argued that victims' interests have 'become hijacked by the traditional criminal justice agenda', with victims' causes being appropriated to promote particular standpoints in the punishment and rehabilitation of offenders (Reeves and Mulley, 2000, p 144). On this claim, Sanders has argued that the 'idealised interests and views of victims' have been 'used to legitimate punitive segregation' (Sanders, 2002, p 209), with the consequence that 'victims are being used in the service of exclusion' of offenders (Sanders, 2002, p 222).

Much of the scholarly research and writing on victims and the criminal justice process has focused on initiatives to include victims in the progress of their own cases, but there has been far less concern with the inclusion of *victims as actors* in the criminal justice policy process. Given this lack of attention, and given that this book places the victim at the centre of the conceptualisation of 'hate crime', this chapter evaluates an attempt to include victims of 'hate crime' in the criminal justice policy process by an innovative multi-agency forum, the London-wide Race Hate Crime Forum. The inclusion of victims was not in the service of punitive measures against offenders, but to spotlight shortcomings in the response by statutory agencies to 'race-hate crime'. Given the inadequacies of the police response to 'hate crime' discussed in the last chapter, such a role for victims offers significant potential.

'Race-hate' crime and multi-agency working in the European Union

The London-wide Race Hate Crime Forum was established in 2003 with the aim of improving coordination between the key agencies responsible for dealing with victims of 'race-hate' at the local level in the London boroughs and also London-wide. The goal was to identify and disseminate good practice policy learning and to promote a uniform service across London. This chapter draws from a research project carried out from May 2006 to March 2007, which aimed to evaluate the Forum as a model of good practice for multi-agency partnerships in other cities and regions in European Union (EU) member states (Iganski, 2007) (the methodology of the research project is outlined in Appendix F to this book). The importance of cooperation between the police and other statutory agencies in tackling 'race-hate crime', and between the statutory agencies and non-governmental organisations, has long been recognised in European countries. Despite this recognition the actual practice of multi-agency working, and how victims might be included in the practice, has been subject to little attention in EU reports on 'race-hate crime'. Evidence of multi-agency working in EU countries is also patchy in the scholarly literature on policy intervention against 'race-hate crime'.

The EUMC on Racism and Xenophobia (now the European Agency for Fundamental Rights [FRA]) recently proposed in its report, *Racist violence in 15 EU member states*, that 'ethical working practices' are a key criterion of good practice when working with victims of 'race-hate crime'. An important ethical practice singled out by the EUMC is for consideration to be given to 'the experiences, feelings, and opinions of victims' (EUMC, 2005a, p 195). However, there is a paucity of guidance in the policy literature about how victims of 'hate crime' might be included in the policy process. For instance, in the same report, the

EUMC suggests that: 'Although the majority of Member States suffer from a lack of comprehensive data collection and accompanying practical responses to racist crime and violence, examples do exist of "good practice" responses to racist violence' (EUMC, 2005a, p 193). However, in the few examples of good practice initiatives that the report provides, there is little mention of multi-agency working and none about how victims of racist crime might be included in the process. Similarly, in its recent report on *Policing racist crime and violence*, the EUMC concludes that it is 'essential that the police work closely in cooperation with all the other agencies who can contribute to the eradication of racism, especially other public authorities and – most importantly – community groups and NGOs' (EUMC, 2005b, p 45). However, policy guidance, or indeed any information, about how such cooperation should work in practice, and how victims should be involved in the process, is absent from the EUMC report.

Multi-agency working and victims of 'race-hate crime' in the UK

The multi-agency approach to dealing with 'race-hate crime' has a long provenance in the UK. Central government has a substantial record of evaluating multi-agency initiatives and issuing recommendations for good practice. Across two decades of official policy guidance on multi-agency working from the early 1980s, there has been an explicit recognition that not only must multi-agency arrangements be responsive to the needs of victims, but also that community leaders and community organisations representing victimised communities should be represented in such arrangements as partners with statutory sector agencies. The 1981 Home Office report, *Racial attacks*, hailed as putting 'racial attacks on the political agenda for the first time' (Home Office, 1989, p 1), explicitly identified the need for cooperation and coordination between local agencies, and between local agencies and local communities (Home Office, 1981, paras 52, 84, 86). Notably, the research that formed the basis of the Home Office report consciously engaged with minority ethnic communities to take a sounding of their views about the problems they faced. However, the report did not offer any guidance about how multi-agency and community coordination might be organised. Consequently, the reference point commonly used in the policy literature for the origins of multi-agency working in the UK is the 1986 House of Commons Home Affairs Committee report, *Racial attacks and harassment*, which proposed a multi-agency approach as critical for dealing effectively with 'race-hate crime' (House of Commons Home Affairs Committee, 1986). Multi-agency working subsequently became one of the dominant official state responses on the future policy agenda for tackling 'race-hate crime' over the next two decades.

Ben Bowling has provided a far more detailed account and analysis of the evolution of multi-agency working against 'race-hate crime'. He unravels the competing conceptualisations of the problem of 'race-hate crime', and the conflicting motives for coordination and cooperation by the various agencies and organisations involved. He concludes that 'the consensus view that racial violence can *only* be tackled on a multi-agency basis was, by 1986, virtually unassailable'. However, as he also notes, 'anti-racist and police monitoring organizations such as the Newham Monitoring Project ... argued consistently that the approach was simply a "smoke-screen for inaction". Nonetheless the consensus within statutory agencies ensured that the spread of the idea was guaranteed' (Bowling, 1998, p 149).

Following the 1986 Home Affairs Committee's report the Ministerial Group on Crime Prevention established an interdepartmental working party, the Racial Attacks Group, chaired by the Home Office, with representatives from key government departments along with the Metropolitan Police Service, the Commission for Racial Equality and the Joint Committee Against Racialism. The Racial Attacks Group first met in February 1987 and subsequently held 13 meetings, inviting oral and written evidence from organisations and individuals, to gather information about the nature of racial attacks and harassment and actual or potential measures for tackling the problem. It also visited a number of areas to gather first-hand views of the local agencies and members of minority ethnic communities.

The Racial Attacks Group's first report, *The response to racial attacks and harassment*, published in 1989, concluded that although it 'found some instances where two different agencies were working together successfully, it soon became clear that there were very few examples of effective multi-agency liaison' (Home Office, 1989). Recommendations made by the report set in motion a significant volume of specialist guidance over the following decade on multi-agency initiatives, coupled with evaluations of the extent to which the guidance was being followed. Most notably, in relation to the focus of this chapter, the report argued that: 'The involvement of people from the minority communities is, in our view, particularly important since they will have a key role in identifying the nature of the problem and helping to set the priorities for tackling it' (Home Office, 1989, para 206). The report also recognised, however, that for a 'variety of reasons' some people from minority ethnic communities might be reluctant about working too closely with the police. The context for this recognition was of serious and persistent complaints from minority ethnic communities about the poor policing response to 'race-hate crime', allegations that in some instances police officers themselves were perpetrators of racist harassment (as discussed in Chapter Four), and consequent demands for the democratic accountability of the police.

Bowling describes the 'crisis of legitimacy' that had characterised the policing of 'race-hate crime' by the mid-1980s: 'Although the police had strong support from the government, there were strong challenges from various quarters that alleged that they were unable to respond effectively and, therefore, that "self-defence" was legitimate' (Bowling, 1998, p 115). The phrase a 'variety of reasons' for reluctance to cooperate with the police was therefore manifest official 'underspeak'. While the Home Office pursued the policy approach of cooperation and coordination between state agencies and between those agencies and victimised communities, the GLC and other local authorities, according to Bowling, 'rejected the ideas of consultation and liaison, identifying them as a hopelessly weak alternative to local "democratic accountability"' (Bowling, 1998, p 100). However, there was not a united approach by local authorities across London, as some were more positive towards engaging with the police (Bowling, 1998, p 138).

Following the publication of the Racial Attacks Group's 1989 report, the government re-established the Group, and a second report, *Sustaining the momentum*, was published in 1991, which reviewed the extent to which the first report's recommendations had been successfully implemented (Home Office, 1991). The Commission for Racial Equality published further guidance on multi-agency initiatives in 1995 (CRE, 1995). A third report from the Racial Attacks Group, *Taking steps*, followed shortly thereafter, in 1996 (Home Office, 1996). In the case of community involvement in multi-agency arrangements, and relevant to the inclusion of the victim in the policy process, the report recommended that a member of the voluntary sector or a community leader should be given responsibility for chairing the multi-agency group, perhaps on a rotating basis (Home Office, 1996, p 54). The report also recommended that where serious incidents of racial attacks occurred, local community meetings should be called as part of the investigation of incidents, which would be particularly valuable in building the confidence of the community (Home Office, 1996, p 12).

The Racial Incidents Standing Committee was established in 1997 by the Home Office to continue the work of the Racial Attacks Group, and in its report published in 1999, *In this together*, it observed that 'successful multi-agency panels have tended to rely heavily on the commitment of a few individuals. Where high level commitment has been lacking, panels have floundered and turned into talking shops or have collapsed' (Home Office, 1999, p 4). A year later, research commissioned by the Joseph Rowntree Foundation suggested that although 'multi-agency working has now come to be the accepted wisdom for all crime and disorder and community safety matters', multi-agency forums for dealing with 'race-hate crime' had not been established in some of the biggest towns and cities in Britain (Lemos, 2000, p 47).

To conclude this brief survey of two decades of official policy guidance on multi-agency working from the early 1980s to the late 1990s, it is clear that there was an explicit recognition that not only must multi-agency arrangements be responsive to the needs of victims, but also that community leaders and community organisations representing victimised communities should be represented in multi-agency arrangements as partners with statutory sector agencies. This recognition provides the key context for the evaluation in this chapter of the attempt in London to include victims in the multi-agency policy process.

'Race-hate crime' and multi-agency cooperation city-wide in London

In the late 1990s a further significant official recommendation was made about multi-agency working in the UK that had a direct influence over the establishment of the London-wide Race Hate Crime Forum. The Stephen Lawrence Inquiry report published in 1999 (Macpherson, 1999) noted gaps in the 'co-operation, sharing of information and learning between agencies', and recommended that a degree of multi-agency cooperation and information exchange be included as one of a number of performance indicators in a Ministerial Priority to be established for all police services, with the aim of increasing trust and confidence in policing among minority ethnic communities (Macpherson, 1999, p 327). The Metropolitan Police Authority formed a working group to consider the Inquiry's recommendation, with representatives from agencies covering the statutory and voluntary sectors, local and London-wide. (The Metropolitan Police Authority is an independent statutory body established in July 2000 by the 1999 Greater London Authority Act. It scrutinises and supports the work of the Metropolitan Police Service.) The working group recommended a permanent forum to provide leadership and guidance on dealing with 'race-hate crime' in the capital. Consequently, the London-wide Race Hate Crime Forum was formally launched at a meeting in the House of Commons in May 2003 (see 'London-wide Race Hate Crime Forum House of Commons Launch', Metropolitan Police Authority, press release, 13 May 2003: www.mpa.gov.uk/partnerships/rhcf/default.htm). The membership of the Forum itself is structured on the basis of a multi-agency partnership drawn from the key agencies that have a London-wide remit in dealing with 'race-hate crime', principally, the Metropolitan Police Service, the CPS, the Government Office for London, the London Probation Service and the Greater London Authority. Members have also been drawn from the non-statutory sector, providing a mix of governmental and non-governmental organisations.

The core of the work of the Forum has involved the key statutory agencies responsible for dealing with 'race-hate crime' at the local level in the London boroughs making presentations to the Forum about their progress in tackling racist incidents. The presentations have provided a mechanism whereby practice and performance by the statutory agencies can be interrogated and scrutinised systematically borough by borough by the Forum members. While the composition of the London-wide Race Hate Crime Forum is by no means unique in terms of multi-agency working in the UK, the borough presentations have arguably provided the definitive innovation of the Forum. The presentations began in early 2004 with a selection of eight boroughs that had the highest reported levels of racist incidents for the years April 2002 to April 2004 according to police records. By the end of 2007 all the London boroughs had been invited to make presentations to the Forum.

The process of planning and preparing for the presentations was highly choreographed by the Forum staff, and the presentations themselves were carefully staged performances. Importantly, the preparation involved for the presentation provided a valuable opportunity for the borough for an audit and review of multi-agency working arrangements and of services dealing with 'race-hate crime' in their locality, and in some instances a stimulus for action by the participating agencies. With regard to policing, it was suggested by one member of the Forum that:

> "Candidly speaking, on the list of policing priorities and various political influences ... 'hate crime' is not at the top by any stretch of the imagination. Obviously over the last few years it has been very much street crime, street robberies

– that kind of thing. And 'hate crime', and indeed domestic
violence, tends to be lower on the agenda."

This sentiment echoes the findings of a recent Home Office research
study of the impact of the Stephen Lawrence Inquiry on policing. On
the one hand, the study concluded that although the evidence was
variable, significant progress had been made by police forces in dealing
with 'hate crime', with the Lawrence Inquiry seemingly providing an
important impetus for change. The most significant structural changes
in police forces noted by the research are evident in the Metropolitan
Police Service (Foster et al, 2005, p 92), as described by Hall's research at
New Scotland Yard (Hall, 2005). On the other hand, the Home Office
study also observed the continuing low status of police work on 'hate
crime' and even in the study's three case study sites in the Metropolitan
Police Service 'it was commonly felt such work was not perceived to
be "real police work" ... CSU [Community Support Unit] staff felt
their work was not valued in the wider policing environment.... It was
widely disparaged as "pink and fluffy" in contrast to the "glamorous
and sexy" work in other departments' (Foster et al, 2005, p 91).

Despite the considerable policy exhortation for intelligence-led
policing it was suggested by one of the Forum's members that at the
local level police forces in the London boroughs were not adequately
analysing and utilising their data on 'race-hate crime' for intelligence
purposes, and preparation for the presentation provided the impetus
for them to swing into action:

> "Most boroughs don't really look at their profile of 'hate
> crime' until they start preparing for the presentation for the
> forum. Some do, but a lot of them don't. In fact there was a
> borough commander who came up a few months ago who
> said that until they went through the process, they didn't
> really understand what the problem was in the borough....
> It's hard to generalise but I would say that the data and
> intelligence is there but it's not looked at.... At the borough
> level they have the borough intelligence units and an awful
> lot of pressures on them to produce their daily intelligence,
> depending on what the priorities are, and street crime,
> vehicle crime, burglary and now violent crime policy is a
> key thing. There's not a lot of scope, or capacity to do the
> same with 'hate crime'.... The information is there but the
> priority is not there for them to do it ... how on earth are
> you going to tackle 'hate crime' if you are purely reactively

dealing with it – there's an allegation of crime and you investigate it. You must do some kind of proactive research, some informed policing work.... I think it's absolutely essential and it should inform borough policies."

With regard to the presentations made to the Forum by the boroughs, it was evident that they were polished and carefully staged events, for as one respondent from the police suggested:

"Borough commanders don't want to go to forums like this to be made to look wanting. They want to go and look professional and so does the team. For that, there's lots of work that goes in beforehand."

Presentation meetings were perceived by some respondents from the boroughs as adversarial events, given the challenging manner in which some Forum members were reported to have engaged with those presenting. A further challenge involved the inclusion of an account of a victim's experience of 'race-hate crime' and their subsequent experience with the statutory agencies involved in their case. One member of the Forum was quite blunt about the value of the victim's perspective:

"What's the whole point if you are not going to speak to the victims and find out how they are feeling and what's going on? This is alright at the very top and maybe these people have good intentions. The borough commander and chief execs have good intentions but it's at the ground roots. What is happening when they are presented with a victim of racial harassment? They don't deal with it. They don't have an idea who deals with it. It's at grassroots level."

In the words of another Forum member, the account of the victim's experience served as a 'reality check' on the presentation:

"So what we have is a well-written presentation and then we have the reality with a victim in situ. For the most part we have tried to ensure that we have a live individual there: it's not always possible and if not we try to have a representative.... What we do is we try and ensure a balance. So we have the presentation and lots of reality on the ground."

The aim was to present a case that was sufficiently longstanding to provide policy learning as a case study in general for the agencies in the borough and elsewhere across London. Ahead of the presentation the boroughs were informed that the Forum would be aiming to present a case, not with the expectation that the particular case would be resolved at the meeting, but to serve the purpose of broader policy learning:

> "The reason we say that we are having those people in situ is because we can use that to be aware of where good practice can be improved and where learning can be gained. We are very clear that it's not about embarrassing them and hopefully they'll see that because we have told them that that's what we are going to do."

Although the provision of a victim's perspective was proposed as one of the strengths of the presentations by some Forum members it was clear that the process needed to be managed very carefully. The practice in one Forum meeting observed in the course of the research was not a positive one as far as the victims were concerned, as little time was allotted for them to speak in contrast to the time allowed for the polished performances by the statutory agencies. The contrast with the time allowed for the presentations made by the representatives from the key statutory agencies in the borough was stark, as emphasised by some of the participants in the meeting:

> "The time allocation wasn't done properly. The council and the police had the majority of the time to have their say.... They get the majority of the time to say how good they are and how they are tackling 'race-hate crimes' as such, but the reality and criticisms – there's not enough time for that. The Forum is there to address the real needs of 'race-hate crime', the real needs from the victim's perspective of what's really going on.... Basically the victim wasn't even able to finish. What he said could have been more succinct but he wasn't able to get half, even a tenth of his story across. I think less time for the council and more time for the victim."

One Forum member observed that:

> "There seems to be a bit of tokenism ... okay we've had a posh PowerPoint presentation, we've had the borough

commander, maybe the chief executive or their deputy ...
a housing officer will be there. They'll do their thing and
that will go for 35-40 minutes, we then have 20 minutes
left. There's the Q&A with the Forum and then there might
be a little bit of time left for somebody speaking on behalf
of the victims, and I know it's partly to do with time ... but
there's not a lot of time for victims to say anything. Some
people say that's not the right place to do that and that's
a fair question. But maybe we should look back and ask
ourselves 'what are we there for in the first place?'."

The provision of adequate time for victims to present their stories to
the Forum meetings was emphasised by one of the respondents from
the boroughs:

"I think sometimes they have to understand from the
victim's point of view that they might find expressing what
has happened in their lives quite difficult and instead they
kept interrupting saying 'look you've got to stop' and 'other
people have to have their say'."

This was echoed by another respondent present at the meeting:

"When you are a victim of racial harassment it consumes
your life, it completely takes over your life. Sometimes they
do go on, but it's the only time that they felt that somebody
was actually listening. Maybe they could have let him have
a bit more time to talk about his problems. I don't think
he was given enough time to talk about his problems.... I
don't think he was given the chance. He did start off and
because he wasn't getting anywhere, he was cut off. With
racial harassment, there is a lot of spin-offs, a lot of issues
that become entangled and I think that maybe he got into
all these issues and was cut off. I don't think he got a fair
chance to speak."

The impact on the victim was clear:

"He came out feeling very upset and angry because he
wasn't able to have the opportunity to have his say. His case
has been going on for many many years and obviously he
has a lot to say and he wasn't given that chance."

Some believed that victims' perspectives should drive the meeting:

> "I think it should be a more victim-led than a council and police-led forum. Obviously they should be allowed to make their presentation, talk about their data but they should do a separate time where victims, if they have grievances, speak about what experiences they've had, what their frustrations are and how it has affected their lives.... It should be more of a victim-led forum, than authoritarian-led in that sense ... where the other agencies are not listening to them it's really crucial and important that the victim's perspective should be the most important perspective than anybody else's."

In addition to the lack of opportunity for victims to present their own experiences to the Forum, some participants felt that victim advocacy groups and those involved in support for victims were similarly denied a voice at the meetings:

> "I feel like there is a lot of frustration from charity organisations who are not able to have their say. It's all very well the council have done theirs and the police have had their time and voluntary organisations don't have a chance to have their say."

This concern was echoed in interviews involving the non-statutory sector members of the Forum, who argued that the Forum was dominated by statutory agencies, with one member arguing that it was entirely run by them. Significantly, although the non-statutory sector Forum members interviewed supported the Forum in principle and were keen to actively participate, the interviews revealed some fundamental concerns about its composition and consequent working.

There was a strong belief that the voluntary sector did not enjoy parity with statutory sector agencies in terms of the membership of the Forum, with the consequence that ownership and control of the work of the Forum was ceded by the voluntary sector to the statutory agencies involved. Participation in this arrangement, for one member of a non-statutory sector organisation, was seen as a starting point to more inclusive working in the future and they would not be content with the organisation of the Forum until parity between the sectors was established. One remedy proposed for the lack of parity was for an equal division of membership of the Forum between non-statutory and statutory agencies, with the chairing of Forum meetings shared between members from the two sectors to give real 'ownership' to the voluntary and community sector. This latter suggestion echoes one of the recommendations from the Racial Attacks Group's report *Taking steps* (Home Office, 1996, p 54). Another proposed remedy was for the establishment of a sub-group of voluntary sector members to work on particular issues of Forum business. One Forum member who shared the view about the lack of parity between the voluntary and statutory sectors in the Forum also believed, however, that the statutory sector should take the lead:

> "I think it's right that perhaps the leadership of the Forum, in terms of administering the Forum, ought to rest with a statutory body as it's recognising that the statutory bodies have a responsibility that relates to preventing 'race-hate crime'. And I think that where voluntary agencies sit is in influencing that agenda and working in partnership with the statutory body, but not necessarily owning it as their lead responsibility."

For this Forum member, while the expertise of the voluntary sector needs to be fully utilised by the Forum in its activities, they recognised that the initial rationale for the establishment of the Forum, in response to the failings of the statutory agencies identified by the Stephen Lawrence Inquiry, was for the statutory sector to respond adequately to the problem of 'race-hate crime':

> "Of course, people in the voluntary sector and voluntary organisations would recognise that tackling 'race-hate crime' is something that they have routinely done even without resources and funding because voluntary organisations are precisely about that, precisely about filling the gap where it hasn't been met and tackling 'race-hate crime' is a gap that has been longstanding: supporting victims of 'race-hate crime' and the lack of response from statutory agencies has meant that the onus of responsibility and care has fallen unfairly to the voluntary sector. Well the formation of multi-agency Forums was about trying to put that right: was about saying to the statutory bodies 'you have got a responsibility to take a leadership role in developing the agenda around preventing 'race-hate crime''."

At first sight there might seem to be a contradiction in calling for equity in Forum membership between the statutory and non-statutory sectors while at the same time calling for the statutory sector to take the lead responsibility for 'race-hate crime'. However, there is no contradiction when the different contributions to be made by the different sectors are considered in the light of the statutory sector failings identified by the Lawrence Inquiry. Paradoxically, however, putting the onus on the statutory sector to take the lead on interventions against 'race-hate crime', to catch up for the past shortcomings of the sector, has the potential to inhibit the involvement of the voluntary sector by dominating the agenda.

The 'silo-approach' to 'hate crime'

The discussion of the Forum's presentation process above perhaps leaves the impression that the presenting boroughs were relatively passive participants put on the defensive while they were being held accountable for their policy and practice by the Forum. Such an impression would be misleading, however, as borough representatives critically engaged with what some respondents described as the Forum's 'assumptions'. The confinement of the Forum's remit to 'race- and faith-hate crime' provided one area of contestation for some respondents from the boroughs, with their views being shared by some of the Forum members. One respondent referred to it as a 'silo approach':

> "This kind of silo approach is just not the right approach. If you are a Black gay out man and you are attacked is that because you are Black, is that because you are gay?... There are a huge range of different equalities issues for people ... and it isn't that kind of silo approach to equalities and kind of White on Black issue and I think there was a strong feeling that that was what they were looking for.... I think those issues need to be discussed in the Forum because it isn't any more simply a White on Black issue."

A view expressed by one Forum member was that if boroughs were to be held to account by the Forum, as they were through the presentation process, then this could only be effectively achieved by scrutinising the performance of boroughs in terms of their own strategic process. The Metropolitan Police Service uses an inclusive definition of 'hate crime' which allows for different strands or groups of people to be recognised as potential victims to be dealt with by the same departments, Community Support Units, in each of the London boroughs. The Metropolitan Police Service 'hate crime policy' of October 2004 defines a hate incident as any 'incident that is perceived by the victim, or any other person, to be racist, homophobic, transphobic or due to a person's religion, belief, gender identity or disability' (Iganski et al, 2005, p 12). This more inclusive approach to 'hate crime' adopted by the Metropolitan Police Service compared with the Forum was made evident in a number of presentations to the Forum, where the borough police services provided data on homophobic incidents as well as racial incidents. It did not make sense therefore for some participants from the Forum to be focusing on some, but not all, groups of victims. From the perspective of one of those participants, in the absence of such an inclusive approach the Forum itself was guilty of unwitting exclusion, betraying the legacy of the Lawrence Inquiry that drew attention to 'unwitting prejudice' in its highly publicised conclusion about 'institutional racism' affecting the Metropolitan Police Service. The exclusion on the part of the Forum was emphasised by one of the Forum members:

> "Homophobic 'hate crime' is alluded to but not really dealt with. Transphobic doesn't even come on the radar. 'Hate crime' against women, I'm thinking about rape and domestic violence, is kind of spoken about, but there's not very much there. I know that we are largely a 'race-hate crime' Forum, but, and it's a really big but, there are huge areas of 'hate crime' that we don't even begin to think about.... My main concern is that there is nothing like the same attention being addressed to homophobia and transphobic. There is no attention addressed to disability. Women's issues are coming more to the fore...."

The Forum member acknowledged that the Macpherson report (1999) and its recommendation about multi-agency working had provided the impetus for the establishment of the London-wide Race Hate Crime Forum, but they pointed to statutory imperatives behind addressing the victimisation of other targeted communities:

> "We've largely been driven by a combination of Macpherson and the 'race' duty under the 2000 Race Relations Amendment Act. We've now got two more duties, disability and gender, and we are going to have to accommodate

them as the law requires us to and so at some stage the MPA [Metropolitan Police Authority] or one of the other criminal justice agencies is going to have to say 'look we have done quite a lot under the 'race' duty ... but we are not doing anything on gender and disability, what are we going to do about that'. Coming up fast on the inside is the duty under the Single Equality Act in relation to sexual orientation and religion and although religion is beginning to get involved in the Race Hate Crime Forum in my mind it's only coming because it's been linked to 'race'. So we are looking at Muslims, aren't we, let's face it. We are not looking at Jews, we are not looking at Hindu people...."

However, the same Forum member believed that there would be some difficult challenges in extending the remit of the Forum:

"When you are looking at homophobic 'hate crime' in London you are looking at Black-on-Black and Black-on-White and I am not sure whether the Forum is entirely able to focus on the fact that there are Black Londoners who are perpetrating 'hate crime' because at the moment Black people are the victims not the perpetrators.... There are Black men and women who are beating up, abusing and hurting gay Black and White people. I think that a bit of a shift is going to have to take place in people's minds that there are Black people who are perpetrators of victims.... I think judging by some of the things I've heard some people are going to find that difficult just to make that adjustment."

Other Forum members believed that the extension of the Forum's remit beyond 'race and faith-hate crime' would dilute its work and result in different groups competing with others for time on the Forum's agenda, believing instead that the Metropolitan Police Authority should establish separate arrangements for other targeted communities. The continued focus on 'race-hate crime' was important from the perspective of one respondent, as even though they believed that there was considerable goodwill by the government following the Macpherson Inquiry to implement its recommendations, progress had begun to be diverted by the 'war on terror'.

Another Forum member believed that efforts to extend the remit of the Forum to all communities victimised by 'hate crime' did not 'take account of the reality on the ground', and argued strongly for maintaining the focus on 'race-hate crime':

> "I think you need a specific focus around 'race' equality as you need a specific focus around other areas of 'hate crime'. They are distinct in their culture of violence and intimidation and harassment. One needs to have specific partnerships with those communities in order to tackle them. And one needs an entirely clear focus of activity in driving it down, driving incidents of 'race-hate' down.... My own view is that a 'race' equality focus is precisely what's needed and it's that that's proven to be most effective."

Some commonalities between incidents were recognised by this respondent but they argued that different victimised communities have specific needs:

> "Now the perpetrators may share some characteristics, some offender profiles, but the work in terms of reassurance requires you to be specific with that community. That to me is a bottom-up approach that requires that you have that specificity at the 'race-hate crime' forum and it stands distinctly alone. How you then bring it together I think is a question worth asking with other fora and how there is a cross-pollination of best practice and ideas with those other fora is absolutely critical and should be factored in, but not at the cost of an all-embracing one-stop shop for dealing with 'hate crime' as that will probably satisfy nobody."

Conclusion: lessons from the London-wide Race Hate Crime Forum

Multi-agency working is arguably now accepted in the UK as the conventional wisdom for dealing with crime, disorder and community safety, and the importance of cooperation between the police and other statutory agencies in tackling 'race-hate crime' has long been recognised in other European countries and in EU policy recommendations. However, it is notable that research in the late 1990s indicated that no multi-agency forum for dealing with 'race-hate crime' had been established in some of the largest towns and cities in the UK (Lemos, 2000). In this context the comprehensive multi-agency provisions against 'race-hate crime' established in the London boroughs appear to stand as the exception, not the rule, for the national picture in the UK. The structure of local government in London, whereby the city's population is divided by the London boroughs into the equivalent of 32 small cities or large towns (plus the City of London), clearly plays a part. Earlier research has shown that multi-agency working is easier to sustain in smaller conurbations due to the smaller number of agencies involved and with consequently less potential for 'confused direction, poor communication, conflict and lack of commitment on the part of some individuals and agencies' (Lemos, 2000, p 48) that might be found in larger conurbations. Despite the benefits of smaller scale, however, local-level arrangements for multi-agency working can be patchy and uneven when viewed from a city-wide or regional perspective. In addition, key statutory agencies participating in multi-agency partnerships at the local level, such as the police, the CPS and the probation service, are also managed and organised at the city-wide or regional level, and a lack of coordination will prevail in the absence of partnerships at that wider geographic level. In the case of London, the London-wide Race Hate Crime Forum has provided such a partnership and it therefore serves as a third tier of multi-agency working in addition to the two tiers of partnerships on service provision and partnerships on policy making for tackling 'race-hate crime' at the local level in the London boroughs. London is not unique, however, compared with some other cities and regions in the UK and elsewhere in Europe, and the Forum offers potentially instructive policy learning for those areas.

With regard to that policy learning, this chapter has specifically focused on the inclusion of 'hate crime' victims in the work of the Forum. Almost a decade ago now, Joanna Shapland argued that 'criminal justice has been seen as separate from victims, with victims being a rather annoying group which stand apart from justice, but to whom we now need to consider creating some kind of response and making some concessions' (Shapland, 2000, p 148). In contrast to the trend identified by Shapland, by including a victim's perspective in the scrutiny process of boroughs, whether by a victim in person, or a voluntary sector agency working with victims, the London-wide Race Hate Crime Forum provides an example of good ethical practice. The research findings presented in this chapter demonstrate both the potentially important role provided by the victim's perspective, but also indicate how the inclusion of that perspective can be one of the most sensitive and challenging elements of multi-agency working against 'race-hate crime'. The participation of victims in the scrutiny presentation meetings clearly needed to be carefully managed to allow adequate time for the victim's case to be presented so that they would not be disempowered by the statutory agencies participating in the meetings, and in effect, be re-victimised. It also needed to be carefully managed to ensure that the purpose of presenting the victim's case was to provide general policy learning on tackling 'race-hate crime' beyond the particular case in question, rather than it being a casework complaint about a particular individual's circumstances. Furthermore, despite the success of the Forum in bringing the statutory agencies to work in partnership at the pan-London level, the drawback of the inequitable representation and participation of the voluntary sector in the Forum's work adds to the diminished role that the victim's perspective may play in informing the strategic work of the Forum, and this is particularly pertinent considering that only a minority of 'hate crime' is reported to statutory agencies who are therefore informed by only a partial picture.

SIX

Conclusions: understanding everyday 'hate crime'

Scholarly writing on social problems spans a continuum from highly abstracted works to careful descriptions of empirical phenomena. The aim of this book has been to sit somewhere in between and apply empirically grounded analysis to further the conceptual understanding of 'hate crime'. It is often the case, however, that more questions than answers are raised when an analysis digs deeper into a social problem. This concluding chapter draws out the key themes of the analysis that has unfolded across the previous chapters and raises some questions that the analysis generates.

At the outset it was noted that even though the police and other criminal justice agents in the UK have enthusiastically embraced the term 'hate crime', it remains a somewhat slippery concept. The main problem is that when the motivating impulses for so-called 'hate crime' are examined, it is evident that the emotion of 'hate' often has little to do with it. But rather than arguing for scholars to abandon the concept, this book has argued that advantage is taken of its utility in providing an emotive banner under which is now rallied a once disparate field of concerns with oppression and bigotry in various guises. This is captured in Jenness and Grattet's (2001) notion of 'hate crime' as a 'policy domain', an arena in which elements of the political system and criminal justice process have converged and focused on the substantive issue of offences and incidents where some bigotry against the victim plays a part. In taking the lead from this way of thinking, and given the ambiguous nexus between 'hate' and 'crime' in the case of so-called 'hate crime', rather than referring to this or that type of crime this book has argued that it is perhaps more useful to think of 'hate crime' as a 'scholarly domain' in which there is an analytical coalition between scholars in once disparate fields of study. As was emphasised in Chapter One, this is not to propose that previous analyses of racist violence, anti–gay violence and male heterosexual violence against women, for instance, should now be re-labelled as 'hate crime' studies. Nor is it to propose that future studies in those fields should be unquestioningly considered as 'hate crime' studies. Instead, conceptualising 'hate crime' as a scholarly domain implies an analytic conversation between scholars rooted in different fields of study and disciplines. Such a conversation is distinguished by a focus on the synergies and differences between different forms of oppressive and discriminatory violence, and their intersections where relevant, with respect to the experiences of victims and offenders, with a view to informing effective intervention, whether that be the use of criminal law against, or rehabilitation of, offenders, and support and counselling for victims. It is in the spirit of such an analytical conversation that this book has been written.

It was noted in Chapter One that the labelling of particular crimes as 'hate crimes', and the establishment of so-called 'hate crime' laws that provide additional punishment compared with parallel crimes, originated in the US through a successful struggle by an anti-'hate crime' movement that emerged in the late 1970s (cf Jenness and Grattet, 2001). Since then, in the US there has been a considerable body of scholarship on the subject by legal scholars debating the apparent conflicts in rights generated by laws which, according to the critics, unjustifiably punish offenders for their bad values. In contrast, and with only a few exceptions (cf Levin and McDevitt, 1993, 2002; Levin, 2001; Perry, 2001; Levin and Rabrenovic, 2004), there have been few sustained analyses of 'hate crime' by sociologists and criminologists in the US, with little analysis carried out through the explicit lens of sociological and criminological theory. To date Barbara Perry's analyses serve as the main exception to this trend in the US.

Because the establishment of 'hate crime' laws occurred two decades later in the UK, 'hate crime' scholarship has understandably lagged far behind the US. But there are clear signs that it is now growing in the UK, judging by the recent writings of some UK-based scholars (Hall, 2005; McGhee, 2005) and new PhD studentships in the field. Nevertheless, despite a mushrooming interest in the UK, and despite the extent of crime and other incidents which manifest bigotry, and the press and news media coverage attracted by some of the most extreme incidents, the study of 'hate crime' is very much a nascent scholarly pursuit.

A decade-and-a-half ago, before the concept of 'hate crime' had begun to attract some scholarship in the UK, Barnor Hesse and colleagues (1992), in introducing their book *Beneath the surface*, which focused on racist violence in the London borough of Waltham Forest, suggested that 'It is remarkable, given the many and varied texts which examine racism in Britain, how very few of them discuss directly the phenomenon of racial harassment. It has almost become a specialist subject in the literature where only a few people specialize' (Hesse et al, 1992, p xiv). The same point can arguably be made today about the study of 'hate crime' in the UK. Its relative absence as a topic of inquiry is most stark in academic sociology and criminology in the UK, which are the natural disciplinary homes for the study of 'hate crime'.

One consequence of the lack of scholarly gaze by criminologists is that, according to Barbara Perry, 'criminologists have paid more attention to the criminality and criminalization of minority communities, than the victimization of such communities and its "sociocultural underpinnings"' (2001, p 33). Given her diagnosis, Perry has provided path-breaking analyses by exploring the phenomenon of 'hate crime' through the explicit gaze of some criminological and sociological perspectives central to 'structured action theory' (cf Messerschmidt, 1997). More empirically grounded analyses of 'race-hate crime' had already been published in the UK (before the concept of 'hate crime' had begun to enter the scholarly lexicon) in the aforementioned work by Barnor Hesse and colleagues (Hesse et al, 1992) in the 1970s and early 1980s, and also by Ben Bowling (1998), who focused on the London borough of Newham in the late 1980s and early 1990s. Both of these works particularly highlighted the background political context of racist violence and harassment in London. This book has aimed to take an approach that continues the strong tradition of analysis pursued by the aforementioned UK scholars, of rooting their conceptual perspectives in empirical groundwork, and it also engages with the more abstracted perspectives offered by US 'hate crime' scholars such as Barbara Perry.

A victim-centred approach to understanding 'hate crime' offending

We might not agree with Marcus Felson's suggestion that 'Students of crime science should stop wasting their efforts looking deep into social structure or the human soul' (Felson, 2002, p 176). But rather than trying to look into the souls of individual offenders the analysis offered in this book has aimed to focus squarely on the foreground of 'hate crime' – informed largely by victims' accounts and reports of incidents to the police and in victimisation surveys. In trying to understand the lived experience of 'hate crime', the matter subject to analysis in this book is not the background causes of prejudice, bigotry or even 'hate'. As argued in the book, understanding the aetiology of offenders' mindsets does not bring us very close to the lived reality of 'hate crime'. And, as posed in Chapter One, the pressing question for understanding 'hate crime' is: what brings some people, but not others, to express their bigotry against others in acts of 'hate'? It was argued in Chapter One that to answer this question we need to begin with the social circumstances of offending, and that has been one of the primary concerns of this book. It might at first sight appear to be a contradiction to place the victim at the centre of understanding the impulses of offenders, and if unpicked, many methodological limitations to this approach could be identified. However, a shift back from a victim-centred to an offender-centred methodology brings its own problems.

Three strands of thought have dominated the earlier literature on 'hate crime' offenders and the impetus behind their offending. Each is arguably problematic. In one strand, victims have been cast as puppets of the social structure. Barbara Perry's theoretical perspectives on 'hate crime' as structured action, which have provided a highly influential contribution to the literature, convey the impression that 'hate crime' offenders are automatons, purposively acting out bigotry that pervades the social structure in various guises. The problem with such a perspective is that it does not take account of individual agency and explain why some people offend and others do not. By contrast, taking a victim-centred approach to the analysis of the situational contexts, or the foreground of offending, does provide such an explanation for the actions of offenders in many instances of 'hate crime'. A limitation that will be obvious, however, is that because it relies on incidents having actually occurred, such an approach cannot unravel why potential offenders are not always impelled to offend given the opportunity or the provocation. A second strand has portrayed offenders as victims of social and economic disadvantage. The work of Larry Ray and David Smith, as discussed in Chapter Three, based on interviews with convicted racist offenders, indicates how some offenders have rationalised their actions in terms of the sense of shame and failure they felt about their social and economic marginalisation. Victims were subsequently scapegoats for the alienation offenders suffered. Roger Hewitt's (2005) recent analysis has made similar points. While such a perspective on offenders is compelling, it does not explain why some people in such situations offend and others do not, and why offenders are not offending at every given opportunity. Furthermore, analysis of the suggested correlations between socioeconomic disadvantage and rates of 'race-hate crime' offered in the earlier literature and in Chapter Three of this book do not show a robust enough relationship to extrapolate from research using small samples of convicted offenders in particular localities to a more generalised phenomenon. Gadd, Dixon and Jefferson (cf Gadd et al, 2005; Dixon and Gadd, 2006) have offered a variant of the 'disadvantaged offenders' thesis in the case of 'race-hate crime' by highlighting the preponderance of offenders with mental health problems and other social disadvantages. However, if we look beyond their small sample of convicted offenders, the situational analysis of incidents that this book offers in cases in which offenders were not apprehended (and it is important to recall that the vast majority of offenders are not caught and prosecuted), there are indications that many offenders are not acting out their social disadvantage but are reacting to situational cues in everyday life to vent their bigotry. Finally, the third strand, in considering the impulses of offenders and as conveyed by the earlier literature on 'hate crime', and what might be called the 'extremism thesis' has been dominant in the academic and policy literature and in press reporting of 'hate crime'. While it would be overly simplistic to draw hard distinctions between extremists and 'ordinary' people as, after all, extremists have their ordinary lives too, issue is taken in Chapter Two with the view that 'hate crime' offenders are out-and-out bigots, hate-fuelled individuals who subscribe to racist, antisemitic, homophobic, and other bigoted views, and who, in exercising their extreme hatred, target their victims in premeditated violent attacks.

The preoccupation of earlier research with convicted offenders only conveys a small and skewed part of the picture and it neglects the vast majority of 'hate crime' offenders who do not come into contact with the criminal justice system. The standpoint of this book is that there is not just one type of offender, and each of the types mentioned above are clearly present in the population of offenders as evidenced by earlier research. However, this book aims to add another piece to the analytic jigsaw by using the testimony of victims to demonstrate that many offenders are just ordinary people who offend in the context of their ordinary lives. In other words, they are not far-right extremists, not people scapegoating others because of their own deprivations, and not people suffering from mental health and other social problems, but instead they are ordinary people reacting to situational cues in the course of their normal daily lives and acting out values and attitudes that permeate the social structure. It is the ordinariness of the incidents and the perpetrators that is striking, but also extremely discomforting. For Rae Sibbitt, writing over a decade ago, this discomfiture was one of the reasons why there had been little research into the perpetrators of racist violence. Sibbitt proposed that there 'is some tension between perceiving the perpetrators of racial harassment as violent and dangerous political extremists, and the boy (or girl or man or woman) next door who may be a little too close to home for comfort' (1997, p 3). The consequence, in Sibbitt's view, is that 'it has sometimes been easier to forget the perpetrators and focus on the victims instead' (Sibbitt, 1997, p 3). Arguably, after a decade in which research on perpetrators of 'race-hate crime' has emerged, little has changed. The ordinariness of offenders remains discomforting. It is perhaps paradoxically an emotional comfort to think that offenders are an aberration, confined to the margins of society. By contrast, it is disturbing to think that they are nearer the core, acting out the values and attitudes shared by many. Incidents of 'hate crime' provide a barometer of the prevailing strength of those values and they arguably indicate that they are intricately woven into, and integral to, the structural fabric of society.

Many of the incidents of 'hate crime' discussed in Chapter Two appear to have involved random victimisation. However, the point was made some years ago by Barnor Hesse and colleagues, in drawing from their study of racial victimisation in Waltham Forest in London (1992), that the apparently 'unprovoked episode' of racial victimisation 'may appear random in so far as it is not always clear why this individual rather than another was targeted. But beneath this surface level the choice is not random, it is strategic since it is the community the individual is perceived as representing which is chosen' (Hesse et al, 1992, p xxiv). Given the structural context in which incidents of 'hate crime' occur, we might similarly conclude that they are not random at all but a logical consequence of the particular social values that underpin them.

'Hate crime' and the criminologies of everyday life

Elements of the analysis offered in this book closely resonate with what David Garland has characterised as a 'new genre of criminological discourse' that he has coined the 'new criminologies of everyday life', which, according to Garland, have quickly become adopted by government policy on intervention against crime in the UK and the US. The new 'criminologies of everyday life' encompass routine activity theory – of which Marcus Felson, whose ideas and words informed parts of the analysis in Chapter Two, has been a leading exponent – and other perspectives on crime that include 'situational crime prevention' and elements of 'rational choice theory' (Garland, 2002, pp 127–8). The analysis offered in this book was not purposively written in the language of this new criminological discourse as, instead, the conclusions drawn in the book that have synergies with the genre were first inductively derived from, and grounded in, empirical observation and primary data. (In this sense the analysis unapologetically shares what Garland has depicted [1999, p 357] as Felson's commitment to naturalism as a methodology for understanding 'hate crime'.) Once given life, some key elements of the analysis seemed to bear a striking resemblance to some fundamental dimensions of routine activity theory: but there are also some key points of departure. To further develop the analysis presented in the preceding pages, and also to emphasise some of the key ideas offered in the book, it is instructive to draw the parallels and also the divergencies involved when considering the 'new criminologies of everyday life'.

The most evident point of synergy with the new genre concerns the conclusions about the normality and ordinariness of 'hate crime', which has been a dominant theme across the book. Garland has pointed out that the common denominator of the 'new criminologies of everyday life' is that 'they each begin from the premise that crime is a normal, commonplace aspect of modern society ... routinely produced by the normal patterns of social and economic life' (2001, p 128). Such an approach to understanding various manifestations of 'hate crime' is explicated in Chapter Two of this book, where it is rooted in empirical observation and reports about the ubiquity and the foreground of offending. The normality of 'hate crime' not only refers to the situational contexts in which incidents occur, but also to the characterisation of offenders, because a second common denominator of the 'new criminologies' identified by Garland is the perspective that 'To commit an offence ... requires no special motivation or disposition, no abnormality or pathology' (2001, p 128). In the same way that Felson's work de-dramatises crime (Garland, 1999, p 360), this book has railed against the drama of 'hate crime' as often conveyed by the media. And despite the obsession with organised and extremist 'hate crime' that arguably characterises the US 'hate crime' literature, the perspective offered in this book, again rooted in empirical observation and drawing from the accounts of victims, is that many offenders are just ordinary people going about their everyday lives. 'Hate crime' offenders are not an aberration, and the values expressed in offences are not extreme and aberrant, but widely shared and tightly woven into the structural fabric of society.

The analysis offered in the book begins to depart from the 'new criminologies of everyday life', however, in the attention given to the background context of offending, as well as the foreground events of 'hate crime'. Despite Felson's advice not to waste effort looking deep into offenders' motivating impulses, the analysis of the situational dynamics of 'hate crime' offered in this book has been used to shed light on the pervasiveness of the background structures of bigotry, or the collective human soul, that informs offenders' actions. While the gaze of the book has followed what Garland has described as the 'theoretical revolution that would shift criminology's object of study from the criminal individual or disorganized group to the criminal event and the criminogenic situation' (1999, p 362), the analysis of the criminal events of 'hate crime' offered in the book shifts the object of focus to the value systems that inform the actions of offenders. Given the pervasiveness of those value systems, 'the state' and the criminal law arguably play a critical role in intervening against 'hate crime'.

'Hate crime', human rights and 'the state'

'Human rights today have become a secular religion', suggested Elie Wiesel in an address in the White House in 1999 (www.pbs.org/eliewiesel/resources/millennium.html). Clearly, the discourse of human rights has become a dominant paradigm through which international and domestic conflicts are commonly viewed. The matter of human rights necessarily involves the state as the protector of the rights of its citizens, and also, as the case has been all too often, the violator of its citizens' human rights. The problem of 'hate crime' can be seen to be most fundamentally a human rights problem when analysed through the human rights paradigm, as is increasingly being articulated in the policy literature in the UK (cf Horvath and Kelly, 2007), as it deprives victims of the right to liberty and security of the person, the right to freedom from exploitation, violence and abuse, and, on occasion as catalogued in Chapter One of this book, the right to life (Respond, Voice UK and The Anne Craft Trust (2007). Furthermore, state intervention against the problem of 'hate crime' involves the state either as the guarantor or, alternatively, the violator of the human rights of its citizens, depending upon which competing perspective is taken. With regard to so-called 'hate crime laws' it was noted in Chapter Four of this book that a debate has raged in the US between legal scholars, and also unfolded by newspaper columnists, about whether such laws are justified. There have been echoes of this debate in the UK too. As was noted in Chapter Four, critics argue that the additional punishment of 'hate crime' offenders over and above the punishment for a parallel crime amounts to the state criminalising the expression of particular thoughts, opinions and values. As one particularly eloquent critic put it: 'One of the worst defects of hate crime laws is that they punish not just deeds, but opinions: not just what the criminal did, but what he [sic] believed. This amounts to an assault on freedom of speech and belief, and ought to have no part in the criminal justice system of a liberal democracy' (Jacoby, 2002, p 120).

Against this type of allegation, supporters of hate crime laws in the US argue that the laws impose greater punishment for the greater harms inflicted by hate crime, with 'hate crime' offenders consequently getting their just deserts for the greater harms they inflict. That 'hate crime' inflicts greater harms compared with parallel crime is clearly borne out by the evidence from the British Crime Survey presented in Chapter Four. However, it was argued in that chapter that when the analysis digs deeper into the type of harms inflicted, it is often the values expressed by the offender that hurt. In this sense, as Barbara Perry and Patrik Olsson observe (2008), the essential harm of 'hate crime' lies not in its aftermath, or its consequences, but in its doing. As Frederick Lawrence has argued, 'hate crime' violates the 'equality principle' (1994, p 365), a principle that is fundamental to the human rights paradigm. 'Hate crime' is a reminder for the victim of their place in society marked out by prevailing structures of dominance.

Given the ubiquity of offending, the ordinariness of offenders and the structural context for acts of 'hate crime' as outlined in this book, 'hate crime' laws arguably provide an important declaration aimed at the individuals who might offend in the unfolding context of their everyday lives. The persistence and the ubiquity of the value systems that underpin acts of 'hate crime' maintain the need for the law to serve as a cue against potential transgression when an opportunity or a provocation occurs. 'Hate crime' laws are an explicit attack on the background structure that provides the context for acts of 'hate crime'. They are intended ultimately to reweave the structural fabric by legislating morality for the normative compliance of ordinary people going about their everyday lives.

As well as being active in introducing 'hate crime' laws, the 'New' Labour government also opened up a public dialogue about extending the laws to particular manifestations of 'hate speech' more generally. In this context, it is significant to consider, as noted in Chapter Four of this book, that the expressed values and sentiments of the offender play a key role in the imposition of harsher punishment under 'hate crime' provisions in the UK. This is especially so where the values that are expressed that lead to the addition to the penalty imposed for the basic underlying offence are not required to have anything to do with impelling that offence in the first place, or even at all. Furthermore, it is also possible that the offender's attitudes and sentiments expressed in the past, perhaps even expressed by their membership of a lawful but racist political group, can be used as evidence of their motivating state of mind in offences. Given these conditions under which 'hate' is criminalised in the UK, it is difficult to conclude anything other than that the UK's 'hate crime' provisions do outlaw the expression of particular attitudes, sentiments and opinions. In addition, it may also be possible that the basic underlying offence consists of a 'speech crime'. Consistently, each year since the establishment of racially aggravated offences by the 1998 Crime and Disorder Act about half of all prosecutions have involved racially aggravated public order offences with the underlying crimes being offences under sections 4, 4A and 5 of the 1986 Public Order Act (CPS, 2006, p 12). The Crown Prosecution Service in its guidance on public order offences makes it clear that there is no absolute right to freedom of speech, as it states that the 'purpose of public order law is to ensure that individual rights to freedom of speech and freedom of assembly are balanced against the rights of others to go about their daily lives unhindered'. Offences under sections 4, 4A and 5 of the 1986 Public Order Act, which can be prosecuted as racially aggravated offences, are concerned with different ways by which the lives of persons can be 'hindered' by the speech of others. They each criminalise the use of 'threatening, abusive or insulting words or behaviour', but acts of actual violence by the offender are not required for prosecution (www.cps.gov.uk/legal/section11/chapter_a.html#06).

The right to freedom of expression is arguably one of the most contested areas of the criminal law in the contemporary public arena in the UK. Much newspaper commentary has been written on the matter. Perhaps the most controversial type of public expression involves instances where persons are targeted, and offended, because of their ethnic, racial, religious or sexual identity. The use of the criminal law against such speech throws into conflict the rights of offenders to freedom of expression against the rights of victims to protection against discrimination – the same conflict involved in the case of legislating against 'hate crime'. Recently, there have been some high profile cases spanning politics, religion and popular culture. A number of cases in 2006 neatly epitomise the conflicts involved. British historian David Irving was imprisoned in Austria for two speeches he gave in Austria in 1989 in which he denied the existence of the Nazi gas chambers (cf Chapman and Smith, 2005). In addition to Austria, where it is a crime to minimise the atrocities of the Third Reich, other European countries, including Belgium, France and Germany, have also outlawed Holocaust denial. However, it is perfectly lawful in the UK to deny the historical facts of the Holocaust and other crimes against humanity. While the Public Prosecutor in the Irving case argued that Irving's sentence of three years in prison was not enough, a number of columnists in the British press defended Irving's right to free speech (cf Macintyre, 2006).

In another high profile case in 2006, British National Party leader Nick Griffin was acquitted at Leeds Crown Court in northern England on charges of inciting racial hatred. The *Guardian* newspaper reported that, at a closed meeting of the British National Party that was covertly filmed by a journalist, Griffin derided Islam as 'a wicked, vicious faith', while one of his deputies, Mark Collett, called asylum seekers 'cockroaches' and urged cheering supporters to 'show ethnics the door in 2004' (Taylor, 2006). Nevertheless, Griffin and Collett were acquitted. A few days later in February 2006 Muslim cleric Abu Hamza, then Imam of the Finsbury Park Mosque in north London, was convicted of inciting racial hatred, among other charges, and jailed for seven years. The *Jewish Chronicle* reported that in his speeches Hamza declared that Jews control the West and brought Hitler into the world because of their 'blasphemy, treachery and filth' (Rocker, 2006). However, BBC News reported that the Chairman of the Islamic Human Rights Commission stated that the acquittal of Griffin and the conviction of Hamza 'might increase the perception in the Muslim community that freedom of speech was selective' ('Muslims react to Hamza conviction', http://news.bbc.co.uk/1/hi/uk/4690132.stm). That same week violent protest erupted in a number of countries following the publication in a Danish newspaper of cartoons of the prophet Mohammed. The *Daily Mail* suggested that the furore over the publication of the cartoons and the acquittal of Grffin and Collett 'ignited the debate over free speech as never before' (Rayner, 2006).

In turning from politics to popular culture, the dancehall music scene in London has been the site of controversy over the rights to perform of artists who have purveyed homophobic lyrics. The 2004 Reggae in the Park concert was cancelled after intense lobbying by gay rights group Outrage over the scheduled appearance of reggae artists Sizzla and Vybz Cartel, who in some of their lyrics have incited the murder of lesbians and gay men. The 2004 Music of Black Origin (MOBO) awards held at the Royal Albert Hall in London dropped Vybz Cartel, and another reggae artist Elephant Man, from nominations for awards reportedly following pressure from gay rights campaigners. The Black Music Council, a group formed in direct response to the campaign against the artists, protested outside the Royal Albert Hall when the awards event was held (Petridis and Glendinning, 2004). That same year the Metropolitan Police Service reportedly carried out an investigation of reggae star Beenie Man for his lyrics inciting the murder of gay people ('Reggae Star under police investigation', www.petertatchell.net/popmusic/policeinvestigate.htm). Later in 2004 Sizzla was denied a visa to enter the UK to perform reportedly following protests from gay rights campaigners over the artist's lyrics ('Reggae "murder music" star Sizzla denied UK Visa', www.petertatchell.net/popmusic/sizzla. htm). Despite such lyrics, and despite an investigation by London's Metropolitan Police Service, there have been no prosecutions of the artists concerned, and their songs containing the offending lyrics may be bought freely in record shops in Britain.

This brief survey of conflicts over 'hate speech' in the UK reveals that there is no absolute right to freedom of speech, and, arguably, it's a good thing too. Yet it also reveals that the criminal law works in a partial manner, as certain forms of offensive expression escape proscription. There is clearly a clash of rights involved in using the criminal law against 'hate speech'. Such legal provisions throw into conflict the rights of offenders to freedom of expression against the rights of victims to protection against discrimination. Both rights are enshrined in international human rights instruments and the First and Fourteenth Amendments to the US Constitution. The justifications for criminalising expression have been subject to extensive scholarly debate in the US. In comparison, and perhaps surprisingly given the press interest in the clash of rights involved, the principle of criminalising 'hate speech' has attracted much less scholarly interest in the UK, and certainly very little among criminologists. The question that still needs to be grappled with in addressing the troubling nexus between 'hate crime' and 'hate speech' is whether a moral compass can be found to navigate a route through the clash of rights involved when 'the state' intervenes against 'hate'.

Appendix A
The UK's 'hate crime' laws

England and Wales

'Race-hate'

Sections 28–32 of the 1998 Crime and Disorder Act established racially aggravated offences for England and Wales for a number of already existing offences: assault (malicious wounding, grievous bodily harm [section 20 of the 1861 Offences Against the Person Act], actual bodily harm [section 47 of the 1861 Offences Against the Person Act] and common assault); criminal damage (destroying or damaging property belonging to another [section 1(1) of the 1971 Criminal Damage Act]); public order offences (fear or provocation of violence [section 4 of the 1986 Public Order Act]); intentional harassment, alarm or distress [section 4A of the 1986 Public Order Act] and harassment, alarm or distress [section 5 of the 1986 Public Order Act]); and harassment (offence of harassment [section 2 of the 1997 Protection from Harassment Act]). These offences are racially aggravated if 'at the time of committing the offence, or immediately before or after doing so, the offender demonstrates towards the victim of the offence hostility based on the victim's membership (or presumed membership) of a racial group' (section 28(1)(a)); or 'the offence is motivated (wholly or partly) by hostility towards members of a racial group based on their membership of that group' (section 28(1)(b)). According to the Act racial group 'means a group of persons defined by reference to race, colour, nationality (including citizenship) or ethnic or national origins' (section 28(4)). Higher sentences are provided on conviction by the racially aggravated offences compared with the already existing offences. (See www.opsi.gov.uk/acts/acts1998/98037--e.htm#28, last accessed 13/06/07.)

Section 153 of the 2000 Powers of Criminal Courts (Sentencing) Act provides for courts in cases where there is racial aggravation (other than offences under sections 29–32 of the 1998 Crime and Disorder Act) to treat it as an aggravating factor that increases the seriousness of the offence and to state in open court that the offence was so aggravated. (See www.opsi.gov.uk/acts/acts2000/00006--r.htm#153, last accessed 13/06/07.)

'Religious-hate'

Section 39 of the 2001 Anti-terrorism, Crime and Security Act amended Part 2 of the 1998 Crime and Disorder Act by substituting 'racially or religiously aggravated' offences for 'racially aggravated' offences, and 'racial or religious group' for 'racial group'. Section 39(5) defines 'religious group' 'by reference to religious belief or lack of religious belief'. (See www.opsi.gov.uk/ACTS/acts2001/10024--f.htm#39, last accessed 13/06/07.)

'Hate crime' and the victim's sexual orientation or disability

Section 146 of the 2003 Criminal Justice Act provides for courts when considering the seriousness of an offence to increase sentences for aggravation related to disability or sexual orientation where 'at the time of committing the offence, or immediately before or after doing so, the offender demonstrated towards the victim of the offence hostility based on – [2(a)](i) the sexual orientation (or presumed sexual orientation) of the victim, or (ii) a disability (or presumed disability) of the victim, or [2(b)] that the offence is motivated (wholly or partly) – (i) by hostility towards persons who are of a particular sexual orientation, or (ii) by hostility towards persons who have a disability or a particular disability.' The court must '[3(a)] treat the fact that the offence was committed in any of those circumstances as an aggravating factor, and [3(b)] must state in open court that the offence was committed in such circumstances.' 'Disability' is defined as 'any physical or mental impairment' (section 146(5)). Any other hostility associated with the offence is 'immaterial' with regard to the application of these provisions by the courts (section 146(4)). (See www.opsi.gov.uk/acts/acts2003/30044--o.htm#145, last accessed 13/06/07.)

Scotland

Section 96 of the 1998 Crime and Disorder Act established provisions on racial aggravation, and section 74 of the 2003 Criminal Justice (Scotland) Act established provisions on religious prejudice aggravation. The 1998 Crime and Disorder Act (section 33) also created a specific statutory offence of racially aggravated harassment in Scotland, by inserting a new section 50A into the 1995 Criminal Law (Consolidation) (Scotland) Act. A person is guilty of an offence under this section if they (a) 'pursue a racially-aggravated course of conduct which amounts to harassment of a person and – (i) is intended to amount to harassment of that person; or (ii) occurs in circumstances where it would appear to a reasonable person that it would amount to harassment of that person; or (b) acts in a manner which is racially aggravated and which causes, or is intended to cause, a person alarm or distress. A course of conduct or an action is racially aggravated if – (a) immediately before, during or immediately after carrying out the course of conduct or action the offender evinces towards the person affected malice and ill-will based on that person's membership (or presumed membership) of a racial group; or (b) the course of conduct or action is motivated (wholly or partly) by malice and ill-will towards members of a racial group based on their membership of that group'. (See www.opsi.gov.uk/acts/acts1998/ukpga_19980037_en_4 and www.opsi.gov.uk/legislation/scotland/acts2003/asp_20030007_en_ 13#pt12-pb1-l1g74, last accessed 25/01/08.)

Northern Ireland

There are no 'hate crime' provisions, or racially and religiously aggravated offences in Northern Ireland, equivalent to those established by sections 28–32 of the 1998 Crime and Disorder Act and by section 39 of the 2001 Anti-terrorism, Crime and Security Act (see Criminal Justice Inspection Northern Ireland, 2007, p 14). However, the 2004 Criminal Justice (No 2) (Northern Ireland) Order enables an increase in sentence by courts for offences aggravated or motivated by hostility demonstrated by the offender at the time of committing the offence, or immediately before or after doing so, based on – (i) the victim's membership (or presumed membership) of a racial group; (ii) the victim's membership (or presumed membership) of a religious group; (iii) the victim's membership (or presumed membership) of a sexual orientation group; and (iv) a disability or presumed disability of the victim. (See www.opsi.gov.uk/si/si2004/20041991.htm#2, last accessed 25/01/08.)

Appendix B
The process of 'hate crime'

The analysis presented in Chapter Two using police records of anti-Jewish incidents in London draws from qualitative accounts of incidents that go well beyond the information conveyed by newspaper reports of 'hate crime'. It would have been preferable, however, in terms of gaining a deeper understanding of the events that have been analysed, to gather information directly from victims, perpetrators and witnesses. Given the conditions of confidentiality attached to the police records, it was not possible to follow up the written records with further investigation. This limitation was a source of great frustration in the research as the analysis of the records of particular cases generated a variety of questions that could only be pursued by empirical investigation. In short, the police records provide 'the next best thing' to either observing events as they unfolded (for which the impediments are self-evident), or interviewing victims, witnesses and perpetrators. The practicalities, and the potential ethical problems, of identifying and gaining the participation of such potential interview respondents in sufficient numbers are considerable, although not insurmountable. However, given the difficulties with empirical investigation the secondary analysis of police records offers great scope for understanding 'hate crime', but the limitations of relying on individual moments, or incidents, to understand the process of crime must be acknowledged. Ben Bowling has argued that 'Racial victimization is, like other social processes, dynamic and in a state of continuous movement and change, rather than static and fixed. While individual events can be abstracted from this process, fixed in time and place and recorded by individuals and institutions, the process itself is ongoing' (Bowling, 1998, p 158).

In many cases, the police records of the anti-Jewish incidents discussed in Chapter Two provided accounts of longer moments than just the instant of the act of recorded transgression, as the movements, actions and behaviour of offenders and victims immediately preceding, during and immediately after the events were also captured. The police records were therefore not devoid of process and the recorded dynamics around the incidents informed the analysis and interpretation of events prompting judgements that they were opportunistic, aggravated, or premeditated, and so on. A more substantial omission from the police records concerned the broader social processes that underpin the incidents that were analysed. The accounts of anti-Jewish incidents in the police records were detached from the local social processes in which the particular events occurred: processes captured in the case of 'race-hate crime' more generally by Roger Hewitt (1996) and Rae Sibbitt (1997). However, the data arguably unravel a wider social process that cannot be captured by localised studies in particular neighbourhoods and localities. The opportunistic, aggravated and random character of many of the incidents covering a spread of locations across London reveals that in addition to the localised contexts in which incidents occur, the common-sense 'antisemitism' that is manifest in such incidents simmers in the cultural fabric of society at large. When some individuals encounter the right opportunity, or when a particular nerve is struck, that common-sense 'antisemitism' is brought to a boil.

Appendix C
Controversy about the extent of the anti-Muslim backlash following the July 2005 London bombings

In Chapter Two it was noted that in early August 2005, BBC news reported that there had been a 'six-fold' increase in 'religious hate crimes, mostly against Muslims' since the bombings and attempted bombings in London in July (*BBC News*, news.bbc.co.uk/1/hi/england/london/4740015.stm). But the same BBC news item reported some equivocation on the part of Metropolitan Police Assistant Commissioner Tarique Ghaffur. He stated that "there is no doubt that incidents impacting on the Muslim community have increased", but he was also reported as saying that "the rise was partly due to the fact that faith hate crimes were now recorded separately from other racial incidents". Echoing this view about the problem of reliability of the police 'hate crime' data, Metropolitan Police Authority Chairman Len Duvall reportedly stated that the classification of many previously defined racial incidents as faith incidents had produced a "large percentage increase from a very low base". To confound the picture even further, the Hindu Forum of Britain claimed in written evidence to the Home Affairs Select Committee (Hindu Forum of Britain, 2005) that Hindus and Sikhs were more vulnerable to 'hate crime' in London than Muslims following the July 2005 bombings, claiming that 'Many of the instances of faith hate crime were due to mistaken identity since Hindus, Sikhs and Muslims from the Asian community look alike'. ([Mr] David Winnick MP put it more bluntly at the Home Affairs Select Committee meeting that: 'Clearly, among certain sorts of thugs in Britain there is no distinction: they are all Pakis, so to speak, in the language of such extremists', and as Sir Ian Blair, Commissioner of the Metropolitan Police Service, said in his reply: 'The kind of idiot that attacks a turban attacks a hijab or a yar mulke for that matter': House of Commons Home Affairs Select Committee, 2005, Q70.) However, the Commissioner was rather more circumspect on the matter of the extent of incidents against Muslims, reporting that:

> ... the pattern does not show very much of an increase. We
> have two categories of reporting: faith hate crime and hate
> crime. The faith hate crime is almost a new development

in the last year, so it has shown a very significant rise. As soon as you then compare it with the hate crimes you will find the hate crimes have fallen in almost exactly the same numbers, so it is a fairly straightforward pattern which rose a little bit after 7 July and a little bit after 21 July but has now returned to levels existing throughout the year. We have not seen in London a rise in attacks of that nature. (House of Commons Home Affairs Select Committee, 2005, Q66)

Some months later in a House of Commons debate on 3 November 2005 it was questioned whether the Muslim community had been targeted at all in a backlash following the London bombings. James Clappison MP, and member of the Home Affairs Committee, stated that:

"Given the lack of information, our judgment is inevitably subjective, but I do not feel that there was an upsurge in Islamophobia after 9/11 or more recent attacks in this country. British public opinion is more sophisticated than it is sometimes given credit for, and people can see that these wicked terrorist attacks are carried out by a very small number of people. The overwhelming majority of this country's citizens distinguish between those people and the rest of the Muslim community, and they feel sympathy towards that community because of that small minority's activities."

Dr Ivan Lewis MP also stated that:

"I cannot think of any instances of brutality or retaliation against individual innocent Muslims since 7/7 by members of the non-Muslim community that have been reported. Perhaps I am wrong about that, but fear is subjective, and the reality of worsening community relations might not be so extensive, or, indeed, may not exist."

Police data shed little light on the matter. In their Crime Report Information System (CRIS) the Metropolitan Police Service has used since January 2002 a 'faith-hate' flag for incidents with sub-flags for the religion of the victim. They define a 'faith-related incident' as: 'Any incident which is perceived to be based upon prejudice towards or hatred of the faith of the victim or so perceived by the victim or any other person'. Following the 7/7 bombings there was a spike in the number of such recorded incidents. It was a sharp, but temporary phenomenon as it subsided by late August to the level of incidents prior to the bombings. The data clearly appear to show a transient backlash. As was the case with the 'faith–hate' incidents, the number of recorded incidents flagged as 'racial incidents' by the Metropolitan Police Service rose sharply following the July 2005 bombings. But the Metropolitan Police Service flagging system allows incidents to be flagged as both 'faith–hate' and 'racial' if the recording officer decides to do so, therefore caution must be exercised in interpreting the apparent trends in the data.

Appendix D
Ethnic group composition of the London boroughs (2001 Census)

	Total population 2001	% borough population Asian	% borough population Black	% borough population Chinese	% borough population White
Barking & Dagenham	163,944	5.38	8.19	0.47	85.19
Barnet	314,564	13.36	7.03	2.03	74.03
Bexley	218,307	3.8	3.44	0.71	91.39
Brent	263,464	28.69	21.56	1.07	45.27
Bromley	295,532	3.14	3.75	0.61	91.59
Camden	198,020	11.38	9.72	1.75	73.17
Croydon	330,587	12.36	15.17	0.67	70.16
Ealing	300,948	25.75	10.24	1.19	58.73
Enfield	273,559	8.6	11.77	0.74	77.11
Greenwich	214,403	7.4	12.55	1.18	77.11
Hackney	202,824	9.36	26.96	1.17	59.40
Hammersmith & Fulham	165,242	5.41	12.97	0.79	77.83
Haringey	216,507	7.78	22.23	1.13	65.62
Harrow	206,814	30.62	7.11	1.24	58.77
Havering	224,248	2.14	1.87	0.40	95.17
Hillingdon	243,006	14.42	4.17	0.77	79.06
Hounslow	212,341	25.86	5.4	0.87	64.87
Islington	175,797	6.27	13.89	1.75	75.35
Kensington & Chelsea	158,919	6.04	8.45	1.63	78.61
Kingston upon Thames	147,273	8.73	2.24	1.38	84.46
Lambeth	266,169	5.36	28.57	1.26	62.39
Lewisham	248,922	4.43	25.96	1.38	65.92
Merton	187,908	12.09	9.04	1.32	74.97
Newham	243,891	33.19	23.49	0.96	39.42
Redbridge	238,635	25.76	8.69	0.82	63.52
Richmond upon Thames	172,335	4.76	1.58	0.75	90.98
Southwark	244,866	4.61	28.06	1.83	63.02
Sutton	179,768	5.44	3.43	0.67	89.20

	Total population 2001	% borough population Asian	% borough population Black	% borough population Chinese	% borough population White
Tower Hamlets	196,106	37.3	7.7	1.82	51.40
Waltham Forest	218,341	15.48	17.35	0.66	64.49
Wandsworth	260,380	7.79	11.22	0.86	77.95
Westminster	181,286	10.23	8.86	2.25	73.21

Source: Census area statistics theme tables. ONS Crown Copyright Reserved (from Nomis on 8 March 2007)

Appendix E
Black and Asian minority ethnic (BME) group population proportions and diversity scores for the London boroughs (1991 and 2001)

	% of the population that classified themselves in BME groups in the Census		Simpson's diversity score		
	1991	2001	1991	2001	% change in diversity score 1991–2001
Newham	42.31	60.58	2.74	4.74	72.99
Brent	44.80	54.72	2.86	3.80	32.87
Tower Hamlets	35.58	48.60	2.13	2.64	23.94
Ealing	32.29	41.28	2.05	2.62	27.80
Harrow	26.20	41.23	1.75	2.50	42.86
Hackney	33.57	40.60	2.16	2.61	20.83
Lambeth	30.26	37.61	1.97	2.37	20.30
Southwark	24.43	36.98	1.71	2.31	35.09
Redbridge	21.40	36.48	1.59	2.32	45.91
Waltham Forest	25.57	35.51	1.77	2.29	29.38
Hounslow	24.43	35.13	1.69	2.19	29.59
Haringey	29.01	34.38	1.93	2.21	14.51
Lewisham	21.97	34.08	1.61	2.17	34.78
Croydon	17.58	29.84	1.46	1.97	34.93
Camden	17.85	26.83	1.47	1.83	24.49
Westminster	21.42	26.79	1.60	1.83	14.38
Barnet	18.40	25.97	1.49	1.78	19.46
Merton	16.25	25.03	1.42	1.75	23.24
Islington	18.88	24.65	1.51	1.73	14.57
Enfield	14.11	22.89	1.35	1.66	22.96
Greenwich	12.74	22.89	1.31	1.66	26.72

	% of the population that classified themselves in BME groups in the Census		Simpson's diversity score		
	1991	2001	1991	2001	% change in diversity score 1991–2001
Hammersmith & Fulham	17.50	22.17	1.46	1.63	11.64
Wandsworth	20.05	22.05	1.55	1.63	5.16
Kensington & Chelsea	15.61	21.39	1.40	1.60	14.29
Hillingdon	12.29	20.94	1.29	1.57	21.71
Kingston upon Thames	8.61	15.54	1.20	1.39	15.83
City of London	7.29	15.44	1.16	1.39	19.83
Barking & Dagenham	6.81	14.81	1.15	1.37	19.13
Sutton	5.91	10.80	1.13	1.25	10.62
Richmond upon Thames	5.48	9.02	1.12	1.21	8.04
Bexley	5.80	8.61	1.13	1.20	6.19
Bromley	4.67	8.41	1.10	1.19	8.18
Havering	3.19	4.83	1.07	1.10	2.80
All England and Wales	5.92	8.69	1.13	1.20	6.19

Source: Greater London Authority

A Simpson's Diversity Index is used to provide the diversity scores. The score is calculated by taking the reciprocal of the sum of the squares of the proportion of the borough population (and in the case of England and Wales, the population of the two countries combined) in each of the 10 ethnic groups used in the ethnic group question of the 1991 Census. (As the 2001 Census output shows 16 ethnic groups compared to the 10 in the 1991 Census output it is necessary to aggregate the 16 groups into the 10 from 1991 [see Piggott, 2006, p 7].) The resulting diversity score ranges between 1 and 10, whereby 1 indicates no diversity in that the population consists entirely of one group, and 10 indicates that 10% of the population is from each of the 10 ethnic groups (Piggott, 2006, pp 7-8).

Appendix F
Methodology of the evaluation of the London-wide Race Hate Crime Forum

The research, carried out from May to October 2006, aimed to evaluate the Forum as a model of good practice for multi-agency partnerships in other cities and regions in EU member states. The research employed an inductive qualitative approach to attempt to gain an in-depth insight into the perceptions of the respondents about the operation and impact of the Forum. Conversational interviews were carried out with 26 respondents who included 16 Forum members and 10 respondents drawn from five different London boroughs. The interviews (with one conducted by telephone) ranged in length from 20 minutes in one case to 75 minutes in another. To facilitate an open discussion in the interviews all respondents were given a guarantee of anonymity in that none of the words they used would be attributed to identifiable people directly by name or indirectly by other means such as identifying their organisational affiliation and position. A participant observation exercise was also carried out in two of the presentation meetings of the Forum. The research used a number of elements of a grounded theory approach to data collection and analysis:

- *Analytic induction:* themes and issues were derived inductively from the data. Given the resource constraints on the research the data were interrogated broadly, rather than minutely.
- *Theoretical sampling:* themes and issues drove the data collection in terms of the research participants and the lines of inquiry pursued.
- *Flexibility:* because the lines of inquiry emerged and developed in the course of data collection no two interviews were the same in respect of the questions asked. Each respondent therefore constituted one piece of a jigsaw put together to represent the work of the Forum as presented in Chapter Five of this book.
- *Data analysis went hand-in-hand with data collection:* and the relevant literature was also consulted as lines of inquiry emerged. The research therefore involved an iterative process of movement between data, analysis, and literature.

A presentation of the research findings was made to a meeting of the Forum in August 2006 and the research evolved in response to feedback at that meeting and further discussion at a subsequent meeting. Following the production of the final report a sub-group of the Forum was established to take forward matters illuminated by the research.

References

ACPO (Association of Chief Police Officers) (2005) *Hate crime: Delivering a better service. Good practice and tactical guidance*, London: ACPO.

Action for Blind People (2008) *Report on verbal and physical abuse towards blind and partially sighted people across the UK*, London: Action for Blind People.

All-Party Parliamentary Group Against Antisemitism (2006a) *Report of the All-Party Parliamentary Inquiry into Antisemitism*, London: The Stationery Office.

All-Party Parliamentary Group Against Antisemitism (2006b) *The All-Party Parliamentary Inquiry into Antisemitism. Selection of Written Evidence*, London: House of Commons, All-Party Parliamentary Group Against Antisemitism (www.thecst.org.uk/index.cfm?content=7, last accessed 26 March 2008).

Allport, G.W. (1954/1979) *The nature of prejudice*, Reading, MA: Addison-Wesley.

Appleton, J. (2005) '"London after 7/7: capital of hate?" The Met's new stats were said to show an explosion in faith hate crimes. Actually, they showed the opposite', *Spiked Online*, 5 August (www.spiked-online.com/index.php?/site/article/686/).

Barnes, A. and Ephross, P.H. (1994). 'The impact of hate violence on victims – emotional and behavioural responses to attacks', *Social Work*, vol 39, no 3, pp 247-51.

Björgo, T. (ed) (1995) *Terror from the extreme right*, London: Frank Cass.

Björgo, T. and Witte, R. (eds) (1993) *Racist violence in Europe*, Basingstoke: Macmillan.

Bowling, B. (1993) 'Racial harassment and the process of victimisation: conceptual and methodological implications for the local crime survey', *British Journal of Criminology*, vol 33, pp 231-50.

Bowling, B. (1998) *Violent racism. Victimization, policing and social context*, Oxford: Clarendon Press.

Brimicombe, A.J., Martin, P.R., Sampson, A. and Tsui, H.Y. (2001) 'An analysis of the role of neighborhood ethnic composition in the geographical distribution of racially motivated incidents', *British Journal of Criminology*, vol 41, pp 293-308.

Bruce, T. (2001) *The new thought police*, New York, NY: Three Rivers Press.

Burney, E. (2003) 'Using the law on racially aggravated offences', *Criminal Law Review*, January, pp 28-36.

Burney, E. and Rose, G. (2002) *Racist offences: How is the law working?*, Home Office Research Study 244, London: Home Office.

Burton, N. (2008) 'Joy as "feral" killers locked up for life', *The Northern Echo*, 1 March, 2008 (www.thenorthernecho.co.uk/display. var.2085980.0.0.php, last accessed 24 March 2008).

Chahal, K. and Julienne, L. (1999) *"We can't all be white!" Racist victimisation in the UK*, York: Joseph Rowntree Foundation.

Chakraborti, N. and Garland, J. (2003) 'An "invisible" problem? Uncovering the nature of racist victimisation in rural Suffolk', *International Review of Victimology*, vol 10, no 1, pp 1-17.

Chapman, C. and Smith, L. (2005) 'Historian is arrested for denying the Holocaust', *The Times*, 18 November, (www.timesonline.co.uk/ article/0,,13509-1877787,00.html).

Cohen, H. (1999) 'The significance and future of racially motivated crime', *International Journal of the Sociology of Law*, vol 27, pp 103-18.

Commission on British Muslims and Islamophobia (2004) *Islamophobia, issues, challenges and action*, Stoke-on-Trent: Trentham Books.

CPS (Crown Prosecution Service) (1998) 'CPS prosecuting more cases of racial crime', Press Release, 146/98, 20 October.

CPS (2005) *Guidance on prosecuting cases of racist and religious crime*, London: CPS (www.cps.gov.uk/publications/prosecution/rrpbcrpol. html#Section3, last accessed on 17/01/08).

CPS (2006) *Racial and religious incident monitoring report 2005–2006*, London: CPS Management Information Branch.

CRE (Commission for Racial Equality) (1995) *Action on racial harassment. Guidance for multi-agency panels*, London: CRE.

Criminal Justice Inspection Northern Ireland (2007) *Hate crime in Northern Ireland. A thematic inspection of the management of hate crime by the criminal justice system in Northern Ireland*, Belfast: Criminal Justice Inspection Northern Ireland.

de Lima, P. (2001) *Needs not numbers. An exploration of minority ethnic communities in Scotland*, London: Community Development Foundation.

Dhalech, M. (1999) *Challenging racism in the rural idyll: Final report of the rural race equality project Cornwall, Devon and Somerset 1996 to 1998*, London: National Association of Citizens Advice Bureaux.

Disability Rights Commission and Capability Scotland (2004) *Hate crime against disabled people in Scotland: A survey report*, Stratford-upon-Avon: Disability Rights Commission.

Dixon, J. and Gadd, D. (2006) 'Getting the message? "New" Labour and the criminalization of "hate"', *Criminology and Criminal Justice*, vol 6, no 3, pp 309-28.

Emerson, E., Malam, S. Davies, I. and Spencer, K. (2005) *Adults with learning difficulties in England 2003/04*, London: Health and Social Care Information Centre.

EUMC (European Union Monitoring Centre) (2004) *Manifestations of anti-Semitism in the EU 2002-2003*, Vienna: EUMC.

EUMC (2005a) *Racist violence in 15 EU member states*, Vienna: EUMC on Racism and Xenophobia.

EUMC (2005b) *Policing racist crime and violence. A comparative analysis*, Vienna: European Union Monitoring Centre on Racism and Xenophobia.

FBI (Federal Bureau of Investigation) (2005) *Hate crime statistics 2005. Methodology*, Uniform Crime Report, Washington, DC: FBI (www. fbi.gov/ucr/hc2005/docdownload/methodology.pdf, last accessed 22 January 2008).

Felson, M. (2002) *Crime and everyday life* (3rd edn), Thousand Oaks, CA: Sage Publications.

Foster, J., Newburn, T. and Souhami, A. (2005) *Assessing the impact of the Stephen Lawrence Inquiry*, Home Office Research Study 294, London: Research, Development and Statistics Directorate, Home Office.

Gadd, D., Dixon, B. and Jefferson, T. (2005) *Why do they do it? Racial harassment in North Staffordshire. Key findings*, Keele: The Centre for Criminological Research, Keele University.

Garland, D. (1999) 'The commonplace and the catastrophic: interpretations of crime in late modernity', *Theoretical Criminology*, vol 3, no 3, pp 353-64.

Garland, D. (2001) *The culture of control: Crime and social order in late modernity*, Oxford: Clarendon Press.

Gerstenfeld, P.B. and Grant, D.R. (eds) (2004) *Crimes of hate: Selected readings*, Thousand Oaks, CA: Sage.

Gey, S.G. (1997) 'What if *Wisconsin v Mitchell* had involved Martin Luther King Jnr? The constitutional flaws of hate crime enhancement statutes', *George Washington Law Review*, vol 65, pp 1014-70.

Giddens, A. (1979) *Central problems in social theory: Action, structure and contradiction in social analysis*, London: Macmillan.

Giddens, A. (1984) *The constitution of society: Outline theory of structuration*, Cambridge: Polity Press.

GLC (Greater London Council) (1984) *Racial harassment in London*, London: Police Committee, GLC.

Goodall, K., Choudri, R., Barbour, R. and Hilton, S. (2004) *The policing of racist incidents in Strathclyde*, Glasgow: University of Glasgow.

Gordon, P. (1986) *Racial violence and harassment*, London: Runnymede Trust.

Gordon, P. (1994) 'Racist harassment and violence', in E.A. Stanko (ed) *Perspectives on violence*, London: Quartet, pp 46-53.

Graham, D. (2005) 'A snapshot profile of London's Jewish population', in P. Iganski, V. Kielinger and S. Paterson, *Hate crimes against London's Jews*, London: Institute for Jewish Policy Research, Appendix A: pp 83-98.

Gramsci, A. (1971) *Selections from the prison notebooks of Antonio Gramsci* (edited and translated by Q. Hoare and G. Nowell Smith), London: Lawrence and Wishart.

Grant, C., Harvey, A., Bolling, K. and Clemens, S. (2006) *2004–05 British Crime Survey (England and Wales): Technical report Volume 1*, London: Home Office, Crime Reduction and Community Safety Group.

Green, D.P., Strolovitch, D.Z. and Wong, J.S. (1998) 'Defended neighbourhoods, integration, and racially motivated crime', *American Journal of Sociology*, vol 104, no 2, pp 372-403.

Hall, N. (2005) *Hate crime*, Cullompton: Willan Publishing.

Hari, J. (2007) 'Gay-bashing should not be a hate crime', *The Independent*, 11 October.

Hemmerman, L., Law, I., Simms, J. and Sirriyeh, A. (2007) *Situating racist hostility and understanding the impact of racist victimisation in East Leeds: Evidence from fieldwork in Halton Moor and Osmondthorpe*, Leeds: Centre for Ethnicity & Racism Studies, School of Sociology and Social Policy, University of Leeds.

Herek, G.M., Gillis, J.R. and Cogan, J.C. (1999) 'Psychological sequelae of hate-crime victimisation among lesbian, gay, and bisexual adults', *Journal of Consulting and Clinical Psychology*, vol 67, no 6, pp 945-51.

Hershberger, S.L. and D'Augelli, A.R. (1995) 'The impact of victimization on the mental health and suicidality of lesbian, gay, and bisexual youth', *Developmental Psychology*, vol 31, pp 65-74.

Hesse, B., Rai, D.K., Bennett, C. and McGilchrist, P. (1992) *Beneath the surface: Racial harassment*, Aldershot: Avebury.

Hewitt, R. (1996) *Routes of racism. The social basis of racist action*, Stoke-on-Trent: Trentham Books.

Hewitt, R. (2005) *White backlash and the politics of multiculturalism*, Cambridge: Cambridge University Press.

Hindu Forum of Britain (2005) *An initial response to the Home Affairs Select Committee on issues arising from the London bombings*, London: Hindu Forum, 8 September.

Home Office (1981) *Racial attacks. Report of a Home Office study*, London: Home Office.

Home Office (1989) *The response to racial attacks and harassment: Guidance for statutory agencies*, Report of the Inter-Departmental Racial Attacks Group, London: Home Office.

Home Office (1991) *Sustaining the momentum: Second report of the Inter-Departmental Racial Attacks Group*, London: Home Office.

Home Office (1996) *Taking steps. Multi-agency responses to racial attacks and harassment: Third Report of the Inter-Departmental Racial Attacks Group*, London: Home Office.

Home Office (1997) *Racial violence and harassment: A consultation document*, London: Home Office.

Home Office (1999) *In this together. Tackling racial incidents: Good practice in multi-agency working*, London: Home Office.

Horvath, M. and Kelly, L. (2007) *From the outset: Why violence should be a priority for the Commission for Equality and Human Rights*, London: Child and Women Abuse Studies Unit, London Metropolitan University.

House of Commons Home Affairs Committee (1986) *Racial attacks and harassment*, HC409, London: HMSO.

House of Commons Home Affairs Select Committee (2005) *Minutes of Evidence*, 13 September (www.publications.parliament.uk/pa/cm200506/cmselect/cmhaff/462/5091301.htm).

Hurd, H. (2001) 'Why Liberals should hate "hate crime legislation"', *Law and Philosophy*, vol 20, pp 215-32.

Iganski, P. (1999) 'Why make "hate" a crime?', *Critical Social Policy*, vol 19, no 3, pp 386-95.

Iganski, P. (2001) 'Hate crimes hurt more', *American Behavioral Scientist*, vol 45, no 4, pp 626-38.

Iganski, P. (2005) 'Free to speak, free to hate?', in L. Morris (ed) *Rights. Sociological perspectives*, London: Routledge, pp 224-39.

Iganski, P. (2007) *Evaluation of the London-wide Race Hate Crime Forum as a model of good practice between statutory criminal justice agencies and voluntary sector non-governmental organisations*, London: London Probation Service.

Iganski, P., Kielinger, V. and Paterson, S. (2005) *Hate crimes against London's Jews*, London: Institute for Jewish Policy Research.

Jacobs, J.B. and Potter, K.A. (1998) *Hate crimes. Criminal law and identity politics*, New York, NY: Oxford University Press.

Jacoby, J. (2002) 'Punish crime, not thought crime', in P. Iganski (ed) *The hate debate*, London: Profile, pp 114–22.

Jarman, N. and Tennant, A. (2003) *An acceptable prejudice? Homophobic violence and harassment in Northern Ireland*, Belfast: Institute for Conflict Research.

Jay, E. (1992) *Keep them in Birmingham: Challenging racism in South West England*, London: Commission for Racial Equality.

Jenness, V. and Grattet, R. (2001) *Making hate a crime. From social movement to law enforcement*, New York, NY: Russell Sage Foundation.

Jowell, R. and Airey, C. (1984) *British social attitudes: The 1984 report*, Aldershot: Gower.

Judd, T., Morris, N., Herbert, I. and Kelbie, P. (2005) 'Britain's Muslim scapegoats', *The Independent*, 4 August.

Kahan, D.M. (2001) 'Two liberal fallacies in the hate crimes debate', *Law and Philosophy*, vol 20, pp 175–93.

Katz, J. (1988) *Seductions of crime*, New York, NY: Basic Books.

Kelly, L. (1987) 'The continuum of sexual violence', in J. Hanmer and M. Maynard (eds) *Women, violence and social control*, Basingstoke: Macmillan, pp 46–60.

Kirby, T. (2005) 'Muslim fears grow over dramatic rise in violence, arson and verbal abuse against Asians since bombings', The Independent, 29 July (http://news.independent.co.uk/uk/crime/article302280.ece).

Lawrence, F.M. (1994) 'The punishment of hate: towards a normative theory of bias-motivated crimes', *Michigan Law Review*, vol 93, pp 320–81.

Lawrence, F.M. (1999) *Punishing hate. Bias crimes under American law*, Cambridge, MA: Harvard University Press.

Lawrence, F.M. (2006) 'The hate crime project and its limitations: evaluating the societal gains and risk in bias crime law enforcement', Working Paper no 216, Washington, DC: The George Washington University Law School.

Lemos, G. (2000) *Racial harassment: Action on the ground*, London/York: Lemos & Crane/Joseph Rowntree Foundation.

Levin, B. (1999) 'Hate crimes. Worse by definition', *Journal of Contemporary Criminal Justice*, vol 15, pp 6–21.

Levin, J. (2001) *The violence of hate. Confronting racism, anti-Semitism and other forms of bigotry*, Boston, MA: Allyn and Bacon.

Levin, J. and McDevitt, J. (1993) *Hate crimes: The rising tide of bigotry and bloodshed*, New York, NY: Plenum Press.

Levin, J. and McDevitt, J. (1995) 'Landmark study reveals hate crimes vary significantly by offender motivation', *Klanwatch Intelligence Report*, Montgomery, AL: Southern Poverty Law Centre, pp 7-9.

Levin, J. and McDevitt, J. (2002) *Hate crimes revisited: America's war on those who are different*, Boulder, CO: Westview Press.

Levin, J. and Rabrenovic, G. (2004) *Why we hate*, Amherst, NY: Prometheus Books.

Loader, I. (2007) 'Has liberal criminology lost?', 2007 Eva Saville memorial lecture, Oxford: Centre for Criminology, University of Oxford.

Macintyre, B. (2006) 'We can't deny the deniers', *The Times*, 20 January (www.timesonline.co.uk/article/0,,1068-2000977,00.html).

Macpherson, Sir W. (1999) *The Stephen Lawrence Inquiry*, London: The Stationery Office.

McClintock, M. (2005) *Everyday fears. A survey of violent hate crimes in Europe and North America*, New York, NY: Human Rights First.

McDevitt, J., Levin, J. and Bennett, S. (2002) 'Hate crime offenders: an expanded typology', *Journal of Social Issues*, vol 58, no 2, pp 303-18.

McDevitt, J., Balboni, J., Garcia, L. and Gu, J. (2001) 'Consequences for victims: a comparison of bias and non-bias motivated assaults', *American Behavioral Scientist*, vol 45, no 4, pp 697-713.

McGhee, D. (2005) *Intolerant Britain? Hate, citizenship and difference*, Maidenhead: Open University Press.

McLagan, G. and Lowles, N. (2000) *Mr Evil. The secret life of racist bomber and killer David Copeland*, London: John Blake Publishing Ltd.

McLaughlin, E. (2002) 'Rocks and hard places: the politics of hate crime', *Theoretical Criminology*, vol 6, no 4, pp 493-8.

Mason, G. (2005) 'Hate crime and the image of the stranger', *British Journal of Criminology*, vol 45, no 6, pp 837-59.

Mellows-Facer, A. and Young, R. (2002) *Local elections in England: 2 May 2002*, Research Paper 02/33, London: House of Commons Library.

Mencap (2000) *Living in fear*, London: Mencap.

Messerschmidt, J.W. (1997) *Crime as structured action. Gender, race, class, and crime in the making*, Thousand Oaks, CA: Sage Publications.

Metropolitan Police Service (2002) *Racial violence: Understanding and responding to hate crime factsheets*, London: Metropolitan Police Service.

Miles, R. (1989) *Racism*, London: Routledge.

Mind (2007) *Another assault*, London: Mind the National Association for Mental Health.

Modood, T., Berthoud, R., Lakey, J., Nazroo, J., Smith, P., Virdee, S. and Beishon, S. (1997) *Ethnic minorities in Britain: Diversity and disadvantage*, London: Policy Studies Institute.

Moran, L.J. (2007) 'Homophobic violence in London: challenging assumptions about strangers, dangers and safety in the city', in A. Philippopoulos-Mihalopoulos (ed) *Law and the city*, Abingdon: Routledge-Cavendish, pp 77–95.

Moran, L.J., Paterson, S. and Docherty, T. (2004) *'Count me in'. A report on the Bexley and Greenwich homophobic crime survey*, London: Galop.

Otis, M.D. and Skinner, W.F. (1996) 'The prevalence of victimization and its effect on mental well-being among lesbian and gay people', *Journal of Homosexuality*, vol 30, pp 93–122.

Peach, C. (2006) 'Muslims in the 2001 Census of England and Wales: gender and economic disadvantage', *Ethnic and Racial Studies*, vol 29, no 4, pp 629–55.

Perry, B. (2001) *In the name of hate*, New York, NY: Routledge.

Perry, B. (2003) 'Anti-Muslim retaliatory violence following the 9/11 terrorist attacks', in B. Perry (ed) *Hate and bias crime. A reader*, New York, NY: Routledge, pp 183–201.

Perry, B. (2005) 'A crime by any other name: the semantics of "hate"', *Journal of Hate Studies*, vol 4, no 1, pp 121–37.

Perry, B. and Olsson, P. (2008, forthcoming) 'Hate crime as a human rights violation', in P. Iganski (ed) *The harms of hate crime*, Westport, CT: Greenwood.

Petridis, A. and Glendinning, L. (2004) 'Triumph for Jamelia at Mobo awards. Protestors defend homophobic reggae lyrics', *Guardian*, 1 October, (www.guardian.co.uk/uk/2004/oct/01/race.arts).

Phillips, M. (2002) 'Hate crime: the Orwellian response to prejudice', in P. Iganski (ed) *The hate debate. Should hate be punished as a crime?*, London: Profile, pp 123–31.

Piggott, G. (2006) *Simpson's diversity indices by ward 1991 and 2001*, DMAG Briefing 2006/2, London: Data Management and Analysis Group, Greater London Authority.

Pinderhughes, H. (1993) 'The anatomy of racially motivated violence in New York City: a case study of youth in Southern Brooklyn', *Social Problems*, vol 40, no 4, pp 478–92.

Rai, D.K. and Hesse, B. (1992) 'Racial victimization: an experiential analysis', in B. Hesse, D.K. Rai, C. Bennett and P. McGilchrist (eds) *Beneath the surface: Racial harassment*, Aldershot: Avebury, pp 158–95.

Ray, L. and Smith, D. (2002) 'Hate crime, violence and cultures of racism', in P. Iganski (ed) *The hate debate. Should hate be punished as a crime?*, London: Profile, pp 88–102.

Ray, L., Smith, D. and Wastell, L. (2003) 'Understanding racist violence', in Stanko, E. A. (ed.) *The meanings of violence*, London: Routledge, pp 112–29.

Ray, L., Smith, D. and Wastell, L. (2004) 'Shame, rage and racist violence', *British Journal of Criminology*, vol 44, pp 350–68.

Rayner, G. (2006) 'The price of free speech', *Daily Mail*, 3 February, pp 1–2.

Reeves, H. and Mulley, K. (2000) 'The new status of victims in the UK: opportunities and threats', in A. Crawford and J. Goodey (eds) *Integrating a victim perspective within criminal justice. International debates*, Aldershot: Ashgate, pp 125–45.

Respond, Voice UK and The Anne Craft Trust (2007) *Crime and abuse against adults with learning disabilities*, Submission to the Joint Committee on Human Rights Inquiry into the Human Rights of Adults with Learning Disabilities, (www.respond.org.uk/assets/files/Submission_to_Joint_Cmt_on_Human_Rights.doc, last accessed 31 March 2008).

Rock, P. (2002) 'On becoming a victim', in C. Hoyle and R. Young (eds) *New visions of crime victims*, Oxford: Hart, pp 1–22.

Rocker, S. (2006) 'Hamza's extreme hatred', *Jewish Chronicle*, 10 February, pp 1 and 3.

Sanders, A. (2002) 'Victim participation in an exclusionary criminal justice system', in C. Hoyle and R. Young (eds) *New visions of crime victims*, Oxford: Hart, pp 197–222.

Shamash, M. and Hodgkins, S.L. (2007) *Disability hate crime report*, London: Disability Information Training Opportunity.

Shapland, J. (2000) 'Victims and criminal justice: creating responsible criminal justice agencies', in A. Crawford and J. Goodey (eds) *Integrating a victim perspective within criminal justice. International debates*, Aldershot: Ashgate, pp 147–64.

Sibbitt, R. (1997) *The perpetrators of racial harassment and racial violence*, Research Study 176, London: Home Office.

Smith, S.J. (1989) *The politics of 'race' and residence*, Cambridge: Polity Press.

Stones, R. (2005) *Structuration theory*, Basingstoke: Palgrave Macmillan.

Stonewall (1996) *Queer bashing*, London: Stonewall.

Symons, L. (2002) 'Brutal assault', *Jewish Chronicle*, 14 June.

Taguieff, P.A. (2004) *Rising from the muck. The new anti-Semitism in Europe*, Chicago, IL: Ivan R. Dee.

Taylor, M. (2006) 'BNP tries to polish image at Blackpool', *Guardian*, 25 November.

US Department of State (2005) *Report on global anti-Semitism*, Washington, DC: Bureau of Democracy, Human Rights and Labor, US Department of State (www.state.gov/g/drl/rls/40258.htm, last accessed 14 August 2007).

van Donselaar, J. and Wagenaar, W. (eds) (2007) *Racism and extremism monitor: Racial violence and violence incited by the extreme right in 2006*, Amsterdam: Anne Frank Stuchting/ Leiden: Leiden University.

Virdee, S. (1997) 'Racial harassment', in T. Modood, R. Berthoud, J. Lakey, J. Nazroo, P. Smith, S. Virdee and S. Beishon, *Ethnic minorities in Britain. Diversity and disadvantage*, London: Policy Studies Institute, pp 259-89.

von Hirsch, A., Bottoms, A., Burney, E. and Wikstrom, P. (1999) *Criminal deterrence and sentencing severity*, London: Hart.

Weinstein, J. (1992) 'First Amendment challenges to hate crime legislation: where's the speech?', *Criminal Justice Ethics*, vol 11, pp 6-20.

Young, J. (2003) 'Winning the fight against crime? New Labour, populism and lost opportunities', in R. Matthews and J. Young (eds) *The new politics of crime and punishment*, Cullompton: Willan, pp 33-47.

Index